HIGHLIGHT THE WILD

THE ART OF THE REID HENRYS

Bruce Henry

D.M, Henry. Peregrine Falcon on Grouse

HIGHLIGHT THE WILD

THE ART OF THE REID HENRYS

BY BRUCE HENRY

PALAQUIN PUBLISHING LTD.

Published by Palaquin Publishing Ltd.
Warren Hill, Hulford's Lane, Hartley Wintney, Hampshire. England.

ISBN 0 906814 01 4

CONTENTS

LIST OF COLOUR PLATES

Plate No. *Following Page*

In Memory of Michael Reid Henry
(1947-1985)

A friend to many and a family man with wide interests,
including this book

FOREWORD BY KEITH SHACKLETON

Before the final choice of *Highlight the Wild*, there had been an earlier working title for this book - *The Henrys, A Family of Artists.* To this it might not have been unreasonable to add - *In Triplicate*.

Instances among painters of a son or a daughter following in parental footsteps are not uncommon and frequently produce striking inherited similarities in style. But three is rare. Among wildlife painters it may well be unique.

A cherished memory of mine is to have met all three of the Henrys. I knew and admired the work of George the father, long before I met him. This came in the mid-Sixties after his retirement from Sri Lanka; at the time the Society of Wildlife Artists was founded and held its first exhibitions.

By then I had already met David, complete with 'Tiara', the Crowned Hawk Eagle, on his fist. Like Long John Silver and his parrot, the two were inseparable for nearly nine years. Now only one of the Reid Henry trio survives - David's elder brother Bruce. To him has fallen the task of unfolding the family story from early beginnings, putting two generations of work drawn from the wild into perspective and providing highlights of explanation.

To anyone who loves birds, and especially those who paint them as well, it is a fascinating story. The superficial similarity of their work soon gives way to a growing awareness of three separate, personal styles, achieved not so much by differences in medium as by approach and inclination.

George emerges as both mentor and inspiration to his sons - an illustrator first and foremost, with enormous integrity. To him, portrayal of the principal subject was omnipotent. Background was simply background.

David's work developed as a triumph of detail in both subject and setting; as impressive a testimonial for patience and dedication as for eyesight. Bruce comes closer to his younger brother but with differences all his own. Detail is a little less demanding, background that much more important. The last Reid Henry is no less fervent an ornithologist but the only one happy to paint landscape alone; enjoying the company of birds as he paints, while able to resist the urge to put one into every picture.

If the trio have one common denominator, it has to be the quality of their field drawings. All of them are clear and clinically observed. They display consummate skill with a pencil and, most important of all, are lovely things to look at in their own right. They also make me feel very ashamed of my own efforts.

I believe the appreciation of any true artistry is no more than the honest acceptance that it surpasses one's own ability. And that, certainly, is why the drawings of all the family appeal so much to me.

* * *

ACKNOWLEDGEMENTS

'Lord, you have made so many things!
How wisely you made them all!
The earth is filled with your creatures.'

(Psalm 104:24 *Good News Bible)*

This book would not have been possible without the help and co-operation of many people. I felt specially honoured that Keith Shackleton, well known as a naturalist and wildlife artist, accepted my invitation to write the Foreword, and it makes a fine introduction to the book. Another widely-known ornithological artist, Donald Watson, has also made a significant contribution. I value his friendship and his many useful suggestions regarding the illustrative material in this book. I am particularly grateful for his interesting assessment, in Chapter 6, of our family art.

My sister-in-law, Dr. Louise Reid-Henry, deserves special mention for she has generously given me access to my brother's paintings and drawings, to select and photograph whatever I wanted; and she lent me a number of her excellent transparencies of his paintings. Many of the illustrations of his work in this book are the product of her kindness. I am also greatly indebted to David Duncalf, of Downland Studios, Worthing, Sussex, whose practical help and professional advice in regard to the photographing of paintings and drawings have been continually available to me. Always busy himself, he has nevertheless given of his time and talent without stint.

A number of people, whose names are listed below, have kindly given me access and facilities to photograph pictures in their possession:

Mr. and Mrs. C. Buque
Carol Bulkeley
Tony Copeman (Zimbabwe)
Mrs. M.P. Cumings
Mrs. I. Curtis

Mr. and Mrs. P. Davis
Mr. and Mrs. J.W.H. Harrison
David Hosking
Eric Hosking, OBE
Major and Mrs. G. Hull
Graham and Elizabeth Jones (Australia)
Mrs. Jean Jones
Mr. and Mrs. W.A. Jones
Mr. and Mrs. I. MacLeod

Others have given me splendid facilities for onsite sketching. I am specially indebted to Reg and Hilary Smith of the Hawk Conservancy, Weyhill, Hampshire, where I have spent many useful hours sketching. I am grateful to Mr. C.J. Lucas of Warnham Park, West Sussex, for permission to make sketches of Red Deer among his large herd; and to Warren Earp, falconer, who brought his Kestrel tiercel into his house for me to draw, because it was too wet outside! I am also grateful to Jeremy Adams, Senior Technical Officer at the Booth Museum of Natural History, Brighton, Sussex, and to his colleagues who, over many years, have lent me cabinet skins of birds and assisted my researches. I wish to thank the Oxford University Press for permission to use several plates from *A Guide to the Birds of Ceylon* (1955); and Royle Publications Ltd. for their transparency of my painting of a Peregrine. I am also indebted to the following: Neil Lofthouse of the *Reading Chronicle*, for the photograph on page 24; Beckett Newspapers Ltd., Worthing, for the photograph on page 13; Jeffrey Taylor of Reading for the photograph on page 26, the Editor of the monthly magazine *British Birds*, for permission to use several quotations from an article in that journal; and Eric Hosking, the author of that article.

I have appreciated the kindness of my publishers, Palaquin Publishing Ltd., particularly Mr. Harry Horswell, and his wife Mary, in undertaking the publication of this book. Finally, I wish to thank my wife Joyce, who has constantly supported me in many practical ways in putting the book together.

Bruce Henry

CHAPTER 1

BEGINNINGS

G.M. Henry. Brahminy Kites - early work. Water-colour. 1918.

1

2

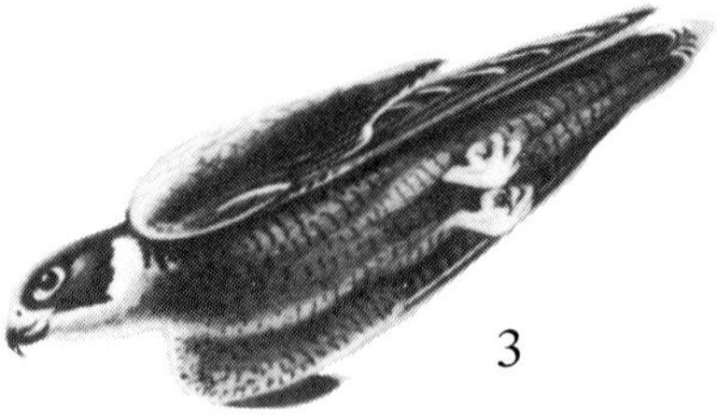

3

One of my childhood memories is of a jungle walk with my father in Sri Lanka. As we strolled through the forest, listening to the sounds and watching so much of interest, suddenly my father stopped on the path, listening intently. We could hear a Ceylon Junglecock scraping among the leaves on the ground not far away. Father took out his handkerchief, made a pad with it in one hand and then clapped his hands several times. It was exactly the sound made by a Junglecock when it claps its wings. Within seconds the bird, thinking that another cock was on its territory, came rushing towards us! It was a magnificent sight.

Our family story begins on a tea estate in Sri Lanka (at that time called Ceylon) where my father, George Morrison Reid Henry, was born on 17 February 1891. He spent his boyhood on various tea estates which were managed by his father, Charles Reid Henry. There were eleven children in the family, mostly girls, and there was never much money to spare. George grew up in a world of beautiful scenery and interesting wildlife. It is not surprising, therefore, that at a very early age he developed an absorbing interest in natural history. With very little formal education he was largely left to his own devices. I quote from his memoirs:

> I had a very deprived childhood, though in some senses only, for in others I had a very happy and care-free one ... Born the middle one of a family of eleven, with all my predecessors girls, and never meeting any other children for play or work, my only pal was my brother Charlie, who followed me a year or two later in the family succession ...
>
> Education was a scratch affair. We started under a succession of English governesses, some of whom we liked — but these generally soon left to get married — and the others were led such a ghastly life that they just faded away. Thereafter, teenage elder sisters, who had had a measure of schooling in Australia, had to shoulder the burden of pedagogy.

Life in that Victorian home was straitlaced and religious.

> By far the most important element in our education came about through family prayers. Each day after tiffin (the midday meal) and after supper, every member of the family had to take part in reading scripture verses in turn — the Pentateuch and historical books of the Old Testament especially, also the Psalms and Proverbs, all unselected and unexpurgated, straight through! We all learnt reading in this way.

Tea estates in Sri Lanka were never far from jungle and there was plenty of scope for the children to roam about and to study animals, birds and insects in their natural habitat.

> The manager of an estate [called] Scarborough, a couple of miles away, was a notable moth-collector named John Pole, who had amassed a very large collection of these insects from many parts of the island, and had added to scientific knowledge no small number of species. Needless to say, to my brother and me he was a hero, and one of our great pleasures was to visit him. He fitted us out with killing-bottles and entomological pins and setting boards and a store-box or two, in return for letting him annex the occasional rarity that luck had enabled us to catch. A huge atlas moth that he gave us induced feelings akin to worship.

1. Eastern Peregrine
2. Ceylon Shikra
3. Shahin Falcon
4. Ceylon Crested Goshawk
5. European Kestrel
6. Black-winged Kite

Monochrome paintings by G.M. Henry (from Plate 21 in A Guide to the Birds of Ceylon*).*

5

4

6

D.M. Henry. Mallards Alighting (painted when the artist was 20). Water-colour. 1939.

It was during his teens that George's great talent in drawing and painting birds and insects really showed. I have his sketch-book with dated drawings going back to his teenage years. They are very presentable pictures, all the more significant because they were the product of his natural, unaided talent. In those early years there was no one to give him technical advice or help.

Here are some comments he made in an essay entitled *Bird Painting*, written much later in his life:

Apart from a very brief course of tuition in painting in oils and water-colour at the Leyton School of Art, while I was on furlough from Ceylon in 1920, I have had no art training ... Certainly I gained very little help in the special field of bird-portrayal (which was the main reason for my enrolling in the School) from the Leyton School of Art ... I already had a natural gift for drawing and had made many attempts at bird-painting in water-colour, but was woefully ignorant of the

1. The Reid Henrys in Zimbabwe, August 1977. Left to right: Bruce, George, David.

2. G.M. Henry. Ceylon Black-headed Oriole - study. Gouache. 1944.

3. G.M. Henry. Metallic Beauties of Ceylon. Gouache. 1935.

4. G.M. Henry. European Eagle Owl. Tempera. 1955.

5. G.M. Henry. Pygmy Kingfishers. Tempera. 1974.

6. G.M. Henry. Crested Barbet. Tempera. 1977.

7. G.M. Henry. Red Campion. Tempera. 1951 (?).

8. G.M. Henry. Salticid Spider (male) - microscopic study. Gouache. 1938.

> importance of composition and of light and shade, and my real gratitude for what they taught me in the way of still-life and landscape is tempered by the thought of the tremendous help they could have rendered had they but realised the special nature of what I wanted to learn.

George's talent was spotted when he was 16, and he was offered the post of Draughtsman and Laboratory Assistant in the Ceylon Company of Pearl Fishers. He lived for several months on a three-masted sailing barque off the north-west coast of Sri Lanka, where his main work was the drawing of dissections and microscopic details of oysters.

> Under my bosses' supervision I made progress in accurately portraying these objects for reproduction by lithography; and in due course my drawings were published . . .

As a teenage lad he sometimes got up to pranks, as the following incident shows:

Bruce Henry. Cormorant on Nest.

Bruce Henry. Studies of Tufted Duck. Regent's Park. 1940.

On one occasion, when my bosses were not looking, I climbed over the bows to the dolphin-striker, holding on to the latter and supported by the bowsprit-stays. In this situation one could watch dolphins disporting themselves a few feet below, before their actions were obscured by the bow-wave; and it was amazing to see them crossing and re-crossing the ship's progress in front of her cut-water. I was thoroughly enjoying myself, but one of the native crew went and blabbed to Mr Southwell, who came on the fo'c'sle, beheld my perilous position, turned all the colours of the rainbow, blew me up and gave me a severe lecture.

My brother David and I were born in Sri Lanka and spent the first ten years of our lives there, mostly in Colombo. I was born in 1918, and David a year later. By then our father was employed by the Ceylon Government as an entomologist. Though based at the Colombo Museum he was sometimes required to go on insect-collecting tours to various parts of the island; and whenever he returned home he used to describe his experiences to us. Sometimes he would draw some of the interesting birds he had seen. In these ways our interest in natural history was fostered. Father built a small aviary in the garden of our Colombo home, and stocked it with birds of several species. That aviary and its inhabitants played a large part in forming David's and my interest in birds. As children we were never particularly concerned with nursery rhymes and suchlike, being more interested in stories of the jungle; and it was a special pleasure to have Father draw something for us. We kept scores of these small drawings, sometimes in colour, and Mother made an album in which she stuck them. It was called 'The Paster' and was a much-loved piece of family property.

On one occasion, when I was in a bad mood, Father said he would draw me something to cheer me up. He painted a House Crow pecking a human toe! At the time, I was not amused; but the little painting is in the Paster to remind me of the incident. The Paster was a considerable influence on our lives as youngsters. We used to watch Father doing the drawing, asking him questions and learning from his technique. At the first available opportunity each of us would do our own bird-drawing and colour it with crayons. Again, Mother kept these early efforts and stuck them in albums, one for each of us. In these ways David and I were encouraged and helped on — and we could have had no better training-school.

At this point I should say something about our surnames. We all had the surname 'HENRY' on our birth certificates, which were written in Sri Lanka. With this in mind, on our paintings we always signed ourselves 'G.M. HENRY', 'BRUCE HENRY' and 'D.M. HENRY' respectively. However, there is a strong 'Reid' connection in my father's side of the family, so that name has been taken by some members as a forename, and by others as part of their surname. That should explain why D.M. Reid-Henry always signed his paintings 'D.M. HENRY'!

Schooldays were a productive time. They gave David and me the only opportunity we had of learning the rudiments of art. We both attended Colchester Royal Grammar School as boarders up to our mid-teens (because our parents were in Sri Lanka); thereafter we went to separate schools — David to Mount Radford School, Exeter, and I to Tettenhall College, Staffordshire. In each case the art department, whilst encouraging our natural talents, disciplined us in various techniques and extended our horizons in the world of art. We learned about perspective, light and shade, proportions, textures and suchlike. In numerous ways we were both able to develop our styles. Even in those teenage years both David and I were able to sell some of our work to classmates to enhance our meagre pocket-money! Occasional pen-and-ink drawings of birds got published in the school magazines. During those years I entered a painting competition in which I won a prize — a box of water-colour paints. I used that box for many years.

Neither David nor I had binoculars in our youth, so wildlife observation had to be by natural eyesight. We did field-sketches of birds and animals when we could, but much of our work was drawn from memory. When Father was occasionally on leave in England we made hay while the sun shone, and were able to learn a great deal from him. I have kept a few paintings of birds which he helped me to finish when I had a problem. This is how the conversation would go:

Bruce: 'Dad, will you help me finish this Thrush? I can't get the wings right.'

Father: 'You've got the primaries wrong. Give me your pencil and I'll show you what I mean. Look . . . the primaries should lie like this . . . next, the primary coverts, then the secondaries, etc. — and, incidentally, you've drawn the bird's eye too close to its beak. Here . . . this is where it should be!'

This kind of conversation, and the demonstration-drawing that went with it, would be repeated time and again, and it was another of the ways in which David and I learned the art of bird-painting. When our parents were away in Sri Lanka (which was most of the time) we just had to learn by trial and error, and also by studying the work of bird-artists like Roland Green and Alan Seaby. We collected picture post-cards of Roland Green's bird-paintings and admired his beautiful pen-and-ink illustrations in books. As for the work of Archibald Thorburn, George Lodge and Wilhelm Kuhnert, it was the ultimate in our admiration and we regarded these artists with almost hero-worship. Another chapter will tell of the influence Lodge had on both my father and David — and, to a lesser extent, on me. All of us knew Lodge personally.

CHAPTER 2

LIFE PATTERNS

Bruce with his father, George Henry, 1978.

George Henry was, by profession, an entomologist. It was not his chosen career but one which came his way through his interests in natural history. I have earlier described how his ability as an artist at the age of 16 led to his appointment as a Draughtsman in the Ceylon Company of Pearl Fishers. That was in 1907. One thing leads to another, and it was through contacts during that period that a new career opened before him.

In 1910 George got the post of Draughtsman at the Colombo Museum, under the guidance of Dr Joseph Pearson, Director of the Museum. His salary was Rs 60 per month — about £2 at current rates! He wrote in his memoirs:

> Dr Pearson was Lecturer in Zoology and Botany to the Medical College, Colombo; and I was allowed to attend his lectures, whereby I received a sound grounding in both these sciences, for he was an excellent, thorough and lucid teacher and I still have my notes with the diagrams copied from his blackboard illustrations.

In 1913 George accompanied Dr Pearson for a further few months on the familiar sailing barque for an inspection of the pearl banks. It was the third and last of his sea-faring experiences, and lasted only two months.

> This was a happy time in my life with interesting and varied work, occasional days ashore, learning a lot of zoology and generally feeling useful.

Then came the big break. In July 1913 George was promoted by the Governor of Ceylon to the newly created post of 'Assistant in Systematic Entomology', Colombo Museum, at a starting salary of Rs 125 per month — more than double what he had been earning as a draughtsman. With this new appointment came much added responsibility and new vistas of opportunity in the world of natural history. George held this post — to which were added various other appointments from time to time — until his retirement in 1946.

To give him a grounding in the classification of insects George was sent to the Indian Museum, Calcutta, under the charge of two eminent entomologists employed by the Indian Government. He spent several months studying insects and learning the science of entomology. He also found other interests:

> Very soon I discovered the Zoo, on the outskirts of Calcutta, and much of my spare time was spent there. The birds especially attracted me, notably the duck aviary with Comb Ducks ('Knobbies' in Rhodesia), Mandarins and Carolinas, and tiny Cotton Teal; also the pheasant aviaries with such unbelievably beautiful creatures as Monals, Golden and Amherst pheasants — creatures I had never even dreamed of. These memories entrance me still.

Back in Colombo, George built up the entomological department's resources in specimens and literature, contributing articles and illustrations to various scientific journals. From all this it can be seen that his appointment to this position was not based on any academic qualifications, for he had none. He wrote with some feeling:

> Being a European, but without university degree or other paper qualifications, and locally recruited and appointed, I had be content with a miserable scale of salary, subject to the whims of the powers that be.

In 1916 George (now temporarily based near Kandy, in the hills) met Olive Hobday, a new missionary recruit from England, appointed by the Baptist Missionary Society.

> Olive Hobday [was] the very first girl I had ever talked to — apart, of course, from sisters — and I soon struck up a friendship ... Before long I was

> taking her for walks about the Ardnaree Estate, and tried to get her interested in my pets, notably the hawks. We took photos of each other carrying hawks on gloved fists.

George and Olive were married in the little Baptist Chapel at Matale in September 1917, and set up their first home in a rented bungalow on a tea estate near Kandy. They had few possessions, but they lived in an idyllic situation and they were happy. Two days after their marriage they had visitors. George described the occasion:

> While delighted to see them, we were somewhat embarrassed because, owing to my having been unable to stock up properly with crockery . . . , we had just enough cups, saucers and plates for our two selves; so our visitors had to have tea out of tumblers and jam-pots, and share knives! However, we made a joke of it and all went well.

I was born the following year and, a little later, my father resumed work in Colombo Museum. He and my mother had great difficulties in obtaining accommodation which they could afford. With a baby, and another one on the way, they moved from place to place in a succession of unsatisfactory billets, the last of which was very damp, ' . . . its mortar and plastering having been done with unwashed sea-sand.' It was in that house that my brother was born on 14 September 1919, and named David Morrison Reid Henry.

Early in 1920 my father was given a year's leave and the family sailed for England. It was Father's first sight of the West. The country was slowly recovering from the First World War and commodities everywhere, notably food and clothing, were in short supply. Nevertheless it was a useful time for my parents, particularly for Father. He was able to get to know his 'in-laws'; and at the Natural History Museum in London he met several ornithologists and also made the acquaintance of Hendrik Gronvold, the bird-illustrator of many publications. He visited George Lodge, whose studio was then in South Kensington. His memoirs tell of the occasion:

> I spent a delightful afternoon with him, admiring the many oil-paintings that adorned the studio and discussing many things with the great man. I had the cheek to show him my humble efforts, which he kindly criticised and evaluated in spite of their hopeless amateurishness, lack of composition and perspective. He recommended me to work on better paper than the cartridge paper I had used; and also to use body-colour instead of pure water-colour.

My father called on Lodge several times during that year in England, and no doubt gained much from those encounters. Throughout his subsequent life, though occasionally critical of some of Lodge's work, he spoke with respect and admiration of the great artist.

For much of the family's stay in England they rented an upstairs flat in Leyton, London. My father tells of an incident in that house:

> We were loaned a perambulator and a cot, and our landlady allowed us to keep the former in the hall. This entrance-hall was papered with a flowered wall-paper which, by reason of age and many coats of varnish, was dark brown, with the pattern dimly showing through; but it was the landlady's pride and joy, and she warned us against damaging it ... On returning home from one of my art sessions I was met by a tale of woe. Poor Olive, about to take the children for a walk, left Bruce in the hall for a moment while she put her hat on upstairs, and he amused himself by pushing the pram up and down against the precious wall-paper! ... 'Mrs 'Enry!' shrieked the landlady, 'Do you see what your boy has been doing?', and out she rushed to visit her best friend and bewail the disaster into her bosom. At which moment I arrived with my paints and, while Olive

> took the pram complete with boys for their outing, I got to work on the scene of the scuffed wall-paper. With such skill as I could command, I matched the pattern in oil-colour, and camouflaged the spot with so much success that when, after an hour, she brought the aforesaid friend to view the harrowing scene she could not find it! Thereafter it became a museum-piece; she took her friends to admire my handiwork!

During subsequent years in Sri Lanka my father produced his book, *Coloured Plates of the Birds of Ceylon*, with a short description of each bird by W.E. Wait. There were 64 plates and the work was published by the Ceylon Government in four parts between 1927 and 1935. This work established my father as an ornithological artist and eventually led to various commissions and other contracts for illustrative work. However, his primary commitment was, of course, in the entomological department of the Colombo Museum, and most of his bird-painting had to be done in his spare time. His next main commission followed after the Second World War, when he illustrated Salim Ali's *Indian Hill Birds* (Oxford University Press, 1949). Later, he produced *A Guide to the Birds of Ceylon* (Oxford University Press, 1955), written and illustrated by himself. It was his *magnum opus*, and a classic which is still in demand in many countries, particularly in Sri Lanka. Much of the preparation for the book was done there, prior to my father's retirement in 1946. My parents then settled in England, and it took another nine years before the book was published.

In England, an entirely new pattern of life developed. Neither of my parents ever saw Sri Lanka again. There was something ironic about this because, until my father retired at the age of 55, he had only spent about six years away from that island. The main reason for not returning was financial; and when, at the age of 89, he was all set to pay a return visit with my wife and me to what he called 'my country', he called it off at the last minute because of a virus attack.

Throughout their life in Sri Lanka my parents had been active in church work. My mother had been a missionary and my father undertook occasional lay-preaching; and when they were invited to accept the pastoral oversight of two small churches in Charlbury and Chadlington, Oxfordshire, they agreed. After a few years in that lovely Cotswold country they moved to Cornwall and settled in Constantine. Another active epoch was about to begin. Both of them served on the local Methodist lay-preaching circuit; and my father was able to pursue his bird-watching and painting, as well as bee-keeping and various other hobbies.

There was a large, two-storey shed behind the cottage. If you climbed a very doubtful ladder up through a trap-door, then stepped on to the bare boards of the first floor, you would see a large room at the end of which was storage junk, old boxes, garden tools and the like; but in the middle of the room was a wooden table on which was a huge model of a three-masted sailing barque. All around lay the tools and instruments, diagrams and plans which my father used in making the model. It was an incredible piece of work. Every single item, tiny winches, ropes, capstans, chains, sails and the helm were hand-made by my father. The hull was carved from a solid block of wood, and the barque measured about four feet long. It is now treasured by the family. Model-making was quite a feature of my father's winter activity; he often made plasticine models of birds, including birds in flight, to assist him with his drawings.

My mother died in 1969 (she was five years older than Father); and in the following years Father paid extended visits to Zimbabwe, South Africa and Australia. On these tours he did a lot of painting, including landscapes, birds and wild-flower studies in their natural settings. These flower paintings were always popular in his exhibitions.

For the last ten years of his life he lived in a flat in Worthing, not far from me. I am particularly grateful for this as it enabled us to confer a great deal in matters of ornithology and wildlife painting. I valued his comments and criticisms, and we were able to share so much that had been denied through the separations which our respective careers had entailed. In certain spheres — specially religion — he was somewhat dogmatic and narrow, and I found it difficult at times to have a reasoned discussion with him; we just agreed to differ! He tended to be shy in company, except where natural history was the subject; then he would enter into a lively and interesting discussion. He devoted a large part of his time in Worthing to the writing of his memoirs. He had kept a diary for most of his life, and found this invaluable for his research into the past. His health began to fail during the last few months of his life, though he was mentally alert till the end. He died in hospital in June 1983, aged 92. He was a man of great integrity, generosity and sincere Christian faith, and his influence on my brother and me was enormous.

I come now to the story of my younger brother, David. After leaving school he got an office job in London for a year or two and was then conscripted into the army in 1940, soon after the beginning of the Second World War. He joined the Royal Tank Corps, and soon became an officer-cadet at Sandhurst. This was not far from 'Hawk House' in Camberley, the home of George Lodge. David lost no time in calling on Lodge, introducing himself as 'George Henry's son', and was made very welcome by the old artist. With characteristic generosity Lodge gave him the freedom of the studio and taught him many of the tricks of the trade. My father writes in his memoirs:

> He (David) spent most of his spare time with Lodge, and became something of a favourite with the ladies of the household, Lodge's elderly sister (unmarried) and his niece (ditto) who, between them, acted as housekeepers. David learnt much from Lodge who, besides painting, initiated him into the art of training hawks and falcons, in which he was an expert of great experience.

During the war, David was sent to Egypt, served in the North African Campaign; he caught hepatitis, which led on to rheumatic fever, and was laid up for a year in the Middle East. He was no longer fit for battle service and was sent to Calcutta as an officer in the Military Police. While billetted there he acquired various pets which he kept in aviaries, and was able to make drawings and paintings of them. His next postings were to Singapore and Sri Lanka, where he had a senior position in the Military Police. While in Sri Lanka he was able to spend some time with our parents and to make studies of the birds of the island. After demobilisation he renewed his links with George Lodge, and was introduced to various personalities in the world of ornithology. My father writes:

> I introduced him to the Keeper of Birds, J.D. Macdonald who, it transpired, was then engaged with F.O. Cave in writing the book *Birds of Sudan* (Oliver and Boyd, 1955), for which they required an illustrator. On seeing some of David's work he was promptly engaged in that capacity; and so launched upon his life-work.

D.M. Henry. Captain Knight's Golden Eagle, 'Mr. Ramshaw'. Drawn from life.

In October 1948 David married Heather Spradbery, and they settled in a mid-terrace house in Woodford Green, Essex. One of the downstair rooms was David's studio, and it soon became full of the impedimenta of an artist-naturalist and falconer: paintings, frames, stuffed birds in glass cases, bird-skins, hoods and jesses for hawks and falcons, art paper, paints and brushes! Pets and aviaries soon began to appear in the garden; David kept a menagerie of birds, including exotic pheasants, doves, hawks, falcons, owls and, eventually, an African Crowned Eagle. The little establishment in Woodford Green was quite inadequate to cope with all the pets and equipment that went with David's career, and when their children came along the house was bursting at the seams. David and Heather had two daughters, Christine and Vivien, both of whom now have their own families.

D.M. Henry. Vieillot's Crested Fireback - drawn from life. Pencil.

David illustrated numerous books and magazines over a period of several years. Those early years were financially a hard time for him and the family. Though numbers of people were keen to employ him with plenty of work, the fees they paid were very low and few of his clients paid promptly. Between 1954 and 1968 David had accomplished a huge amount of work, including illustrations for the following books:

R. Meinertzhagen, *Birds of Arabia* (Oliver and Boyd, 1954);
F.O. Cave and J.D. Macdonald, *Birds of the Sudan* (Oliver and Boyd, 1955);
D.A. and W.M. Bannerman, *Birds of Cyprus* (Oliver and Boyd, 1958);
J.C. Greenway, *Extinct and Vanishing Birds of the World* (American Committee for International Wild Life Protection, 1958);
P.A.D. Hollom, *The Popular Handbook of Rarer British Birds* (H.F. and G. Witherby Ltd, 1960);
C.J. Skead, *The Canaries, Seedeaters and Buntings of Southern Africa* (The South African Bird Book Fund, 1960);
D.A. Bannerman, *Birds of the Atlantic Isles* (3 vols., Oliver and Boyd, 1963);
Leslie Brown and Dean Amadon, *Eagles, Hawks and Falcons of the World* (Country Life Books, 1968);
J.G. Mavrogordato, *A Falcon in the Field* (Knightly Vernon Ltd, 1966).

In addition, David illustrated several postage-stamp series, including sets for Mauritius and Botswana. My father's comments about all this work are significant:

> The task of designing attitudes, unravelling plumage details and patterns, often from badly made skins, and the necessity for frequent visits to the Museum or Zoo, and research into literature etc., can be appreciated only by those who have engaged in similar work.

In 1960 David was commissioned to go to Zimbabwe (Rhodesia at that time) to paint African antelopes. The project proved abortive, mainly because money was not forthcoming, and David was obliged to make a living for himself and family by painting and selling pictures to his many clients. He was away in Zimbabwe for two years. During his stay there he acquired a young female African Crowned Eagle, which he reared to near-maturity and brought to England. He named her 'Tiara'. My father recalls:

D.M. Henry. Kudu.

> She became a dominating influence in his life, colouring it completely as he manned her for hawking, made hoods and other apparatus for her, and studied her intensely. He alone could handle or manage the bird and she had to be taken wherever he went — which included visits to annual game fairs held in various parts of the country, including visits to Ireland; and she became the principal attraction at many exhibitions and other functions — the most

'Show your ticket, please!' - David and Tiara about to board a train, 1964.

9. Ceylon Trogon (male by G.M. Henry; female and background by Bruce Henry). Tempera. 1954-1984.

10. G.M. Henry. Common Kingfisher (male) - Study. Gouache. 1962.

11. G.M. Henry. Curlew, Oystercatchers, Ringed Plover and Turnstones. Tempera.

12. G.M. Henry. Indian Peafowl, Ceylon Spurfowl and Ceylon Junglefowl. Tempera.
(Plate 23 in A Guide to the Birds of Ceylon*)*

13. G.M. Henry. Harriers in Flight. Gouache.
1. Montagu's Harrier - male and female. 2. Pied Harrier - male and female
3. Marsh Harrier - male and female. 4. Pale Harrier - adult and juvenile males.
(Plate 19 in A Guide to the Birds of Ceylon)

14. D.M. Henry. Green Woodpecker. Gouache.

15. D.M. Henry. African Crowned Eagle - study. Gouache. 1968.

16. D.M. Henry. Verreaux's Eagle - unfinished study. Gouache.

D.M. Henry. African Crowned Eagle. Pencil.

> photographed bird in Britain! ... On more than one occasion her terrible talons put David into hospital when, by accident or design, she lacerated his arm.

Tiara appears in several illustrations in this book. She died in 1973, eleven years old, while David was again away in Africa.

David loved southern Africa so much that he decided to emigrate to Zimbabwe. He enjoyed the spacious scenery and the abundant wildlife of that country. He had made many friends there, and had become increasingly disenchanted with Britain. He also liked the warmer climate of Zimbabwe. His relationship with Heather had come under strain for some years, and finally ended in divorce. He had already taken Rhodesian citizenship, and in December 1976 he married Dr Louise Westwater, a knowledgeable botanist and ornithologist who had worked in the Rhodesian medical service for many years. A new chapter in his life began.

David with Tiara, 1964.

David was a very good conversationalist and always had lots of friends. He was dogmatic about most matters on which he held strong views, particularly politics; he was almost vitriolic about bureaucracy, and did not easily suffer others' points of view if they were very different from his own. Nevertheless he enjoyed a joke and told many himself; his laughter was a hearty guffaw, not easily forgotten! Occasionally he had his quiet moments, as we see from this comment by Eric Hosking:

> One day in 1951 I drove him to have tea with the great artist [George Lodge] at his home in Camberley. It was about the only occasion that I can ever remember David being subdued — as they discussed the various merits of water-colour, oil and gouache. (*British Birds* 70: 540-541, 1977)

David had no formal art-training. He learned a great deal from his father and also from George Lodge, but apart from this he was self-taught; and though his skill improved with practice and experience, his style remained virtually the same throughout. He was a founder-member of the Society of Wildlife Artists. He was keen to help young wildlife artists and always willing to share his know-how with them. In Zimbabwe he even shared his accommodation temporarily with a young artist.

Cricket was very high on David's list of leisure-pursuits. He loved to play, despite the potential risk to his hands. In 1973 he was in fact quite badly injured while playing cricket, breaking his left arm and injuring his right hand. However, such set-backs did not deter him and, even while my wife and I were staying with David and Louise — six weeks before he died — he was anticipating a game of cricket in Harare. He was then nearly 58.

David's years in Zimbabwe were very productive and happy — even during the turbulent years of national conflict. He had graduated from the grind of book-illustration and was much in demand as a wildlife artist. He undertook commissions, although he was averse to this kind of outlet, preferring to

D.M. Henry. Flight Study of Tiara. Pencil. 1963(?)

D.M. Henry. Study of Peregrine at kill. Pencil.

choose his own subject and to paint what *he* wanted; but his main sales were through exhibitions and by the sale of paintings which he had planned himself. He held a number of one-man exhibitions in southern Africa and in Britain, and I remember attending one of these in London. It was a sell-out shortly after opening! Ultimately, demand for his works greatly exceeded supply — people were so keen to have one of his paintings that they would leave the price entirely to him! In pricing his pictures he was very fair, though he knew the prices they could fetch; and he was exceedingly generous towards his friends and relations, often giving a painting or sketch as a keepsake. Unfortunately, David did not live long enough to satisfy all requests for his work. He died of cancer after a comparatively short illness, on 26 September 1977, aged 58. He left a legacy of skill and excellence in wildlife art which few have attained.

My birth certificate is a scruffy piece of paper which was written in Sri Lanka. It says that Bruce Charles Reid Henry was born on 22 July 1918 near Kandy. I have recently visited the hillside where I was born, and admired the lovely panoramic view of Kandy and the surrounding mountains. I did a water-colour painting of that view to keep as a memento.

I attended my first secondary school in Colombo — Royal College. A year later my mother brought David and me to England for our main education, details of which I have given in Chapter 1. After schooldays my life went in a very different direction from that of David and my father: I was destined for Christian Mission. Since schooldays I had felt called to the Christian ministry, but was advised, before entering a training college, to gain some experience in business. So, after leaving school at the age of 19, I got a job in a London firm of accountants as an assistant auditor, and spent a couple of years adding up columns of pounds, shillings and pence. This brought in a little money (£1 per week!) and gave me valuable experience in account-keeping which proved very useful in later years. After a short period of military service with the Royal Artillery I trained for the Christian ministry at Spurgeon's College, and graduated as a Bachelor of Divinity at London University. During the years in training I offered for overseas service, expressing a preference for India. Then came a major event in my life: I met Joyce Mary Middleton. She was 20, a student-nurse and she too wanted to be a missionary in India! Within a few months we became engaged and, two years later, we were married.

In the meantime we had been accepted by the Baptist Missionary Society for service in India. However, as the war was still on, passages to the East were out of the question; so, after my ordination in 1943, I accepted a temporary appointment as Minister of Harlesden Baptist Church in north London. I also became Chaplain to the Central Middlesex Hospital and to several wartime factories. During this period London was under attack from flying bombs and rockets; and we

D.M. Henry. African Elephant. Pencil.

D.M. Henry. Crowned Guineafowl. Pencil.

lived and worked in an area of mounting devastation and human distress. Then came the end of the war, and we were able to pack our bags and sail for India. A new career had begun.

After two years of language study we settled to our new responsibilities. We had been located among the Kui-speaking tribes in the hills of Orissa, where there was a growing Christian community. For 13 years we were based at Udayagiri, a centre where there were colleagues engaged in medical, educational and church work; but when a new area was opening up many miles away, we were invited to go and help. We bought a plot of land near Balliguda, built a house and lived there for about nine years. My work had been pastoral and administrative, involving a lot of travelling among the village communities in an area of mountains and jungle; and Joyce concentrated on public health and work among women. Latterly, however, we were both engaged in literary activity. I worked with a team of Indians on the translation of the New Testament into Kui; and Joyce organised the distribution of Christian literature over a wide area. The Kui New Testament was published by the Bible Society of India and is in general use among the Kui people.

We served in India for 23 years, and they were strenuous but happy ones. Relationships were formed with colleagues and Indian friends which have stood the test of time. Our two children were born in India, during the first five years of our service. Michael* is now a banker and lives with his family in England; Carol, also a nurse, married a doctor and they are missionaries in Zaire, with their children. By 1968 our work in India was largely completed, and our family needed us in Britain. We had been able to educate the children in boarding schools in south India, up to the age of about 13, but after that we placed them in schools in England. We were specially glad to be near them when they

* Since this went to press, Michael was tragically killed in a road accident while cycling with his family.

reached the crucial stage of setting out on their careers. Our ageing parents also needed us. It was time to leave India.

But India was in our blood. Its people and culture had become part of us; its wildlife, too. Throughout our time in India I had made a special study of its living creatures, specially birds. I took binoculars and notebook on my numerous journeys and jungle walks, and had plenty of opportunity to study wildlife, not only in the familiar hills of Orissa, but in many other parts of India. It is a country which is largely immune from the pace of Western man; a country where buffalo-carts amble slowly and where goatherds have all the time in the world; a country where people will leave till tomorrow what they could not accomplish yesterday or today! So, despite the demands of a busy schedule, I found ample time for Nature-study; and, when time permitted, I painted. I made studies of birds from life and — occasionally — from dead specimens; and most of this work either found its way into portfolios or was given as presents! I made no attempt to sell anything, for this was a hobby and, although an absorbing interest, had to be fitted into spare time. I contributed to the occasional journal, and submitted pen-and-ink drawings for articles in magazines, and thus kept the interest alive. And all the time I kept in close touch with my father, whose knowledge of birds of the Indian sub-continent was far greater than mine. He and my mother did, in fact, visit us in India, travelling up from Sri Lanka just before he retired, and we were able to do quite a lot of bird-watching together.

I often kept pets; it seemed to be part of our family tradition! Over the years these pets ranged from wild cats, deer and hares to Shikras (like Sparrowhawks), Mynas, Parrots, Munias and a Coppersmith. Just one of the latter was quite sufficient. A Coppersmith (*Xantholaema haemacephala*) is a small Barbet with brilliant green, red and yellow marking, and it sits high in the trees at the hottest time of day, calling a monotonous *tonk, tonk, tonk* for hours on end — hence its name.

I had one of these brought to me and I kept it temporarily in a cage on our verandah. In the midday heat, when we tried to have a brief siesta (like the rest of India), this bird called incessantly, *tonk, tonk, tonk* ... We rapidly went off the bird and gave it back to the person who had brought it! The Indian Grackle (*Gracula religiosa*) is a favourite pet in India, and a great mimic. When I had one of these birds brought to me I promptly installed it in a small aviary built just outside our back verandah. Very early the next morning just after dawn, we were awakened by the sounds of villagers spitting raucously at the back of the house. We wondered who our early visitors were, and got up to investigate. There was nobody about, just a silly Grackle treating us to its repertoire! Our new pet had previously been kept in a local village, and had obviously been impressed by the villagers' early morning performances.

In England, our life pattern changed once again. After returning from India we had to look for a home and a livelihood. We settled in Worthing and started a new venture: I entered the education service, teaching Religious Education in a comprehensive school; and Joyce returned to nursing in a local hospital. After three years in the comprehensive school I was appointed Head of the Religious Studies Department at Worthing Sixth Form College, where I remained for nine years. Again, these were happy years for us both. We were much involved in church work as well as our official assignments, particularly taking a lead in work among young people — our home was always 'open house'. In addition to these activities I was able to lead ornithological groups, in the College and outside, and continue my artistic interests. Love of the wild was in my make-up and paints and brushes were always in use — I was devoting spare time increasingly to painting.

I started to 'fly a kite' professionally in the commercial world of wildlife art. Painting living creatures was not new to me; selling my efforts *was*! I began to find a market for my work, through galleries, exhibitions and private commissions. In

1980 I decided to take early retirement from education and was thus free to give more time to the study and painting of wildlife. In this way yet another career was before me. I entered a new fraternity of naturalists and artists, with whom I had previously only had casual acquaintance; and I was in due time elected a member of the Society of Wildlife Artists. Moreover, my retirement from State education had also freed me to explore other avenues of Christian outreach, in keeping with my vocation as a minister of the Church; and in this capacity I have not only been able to serve churches of various denominations in this country but also to work for short periods in the part of India where I know the people and their language.

D.M. Henry. Unfinished pencil study of Peregrine Falcon.

My interests in wildlife and painting have taken me to various countries overseas, including Zimbabwe, India, Sri Lanka and Australia. Of course, on these occasions I have 'killed two birds with one stone' (a very inappropriate expression!) by visiting friends and ministering in churches; nevertheless these overseas visits have afforded wonderful opportunities of studying and painting the fauna and flora of those countries. I have described, in other parts of this book, some of my experiences on these occasions.

I have always had a great love for music. At school I learnt to play the violin and played in the school orchestra; then, in my late teens and early twenties I learnt to play the organ. Unfortunately, my career in India put an end to this form of music-making — the violin almost fell apart in the climate, and organs were not available in the jungle! Despite this, my interest survived and though I will not inflict my music-making on the public, I still enjoy playing these instruments and listening to recordings. I have also maintained a great interest in sport — like my brother David. During schooldays I was keen on the lot . . . rugby, hockey, cricket and tennis. Later, I dropped the rugby and concentrated on hockey and cricket. I played hockey until well into my fifties, and enjoyed a game of cricket.

Finally, I should like to pay tribute to those who have helped me on my way in the variety of Christian ministry, natural history and wildlife art. Among these my parents take a lead; but I also remember David with gratitude, and others who have left these scenes, including J.C. Harrison, a fine ornithological draughtsman and water-colourist. I am also grateful to a number of living people who have helped and encouraged both Joyce and myself through the years. As a family, the Henrys have been very dependent on the kindness and encouragement of other people.

CHAPTER 3

LOVE OF NATURE

G.M. Henry. Crowned Guineafowl. From colour studies drawn from a freshly dead specimen.

How do you set about drawing living creatures? In our case the answer begins with George Henry encouraging his two sons at a very early age to share his love of the wild. Like father like sons, and George's ability with pencil and brush soon rubbed off; David and I were hardly beyond the toddler stage when we were producing primitive sketches of birds in Sri Lanka. In subsequent years, therefore, it was hardly surprising to find all three of us in our respective situations spending every available opportunity watching Nature. Country walks, whether among the fields and lanes of Britain, in the vast plains of Africa or in the jungles of India and Sri Lanka, have been a crucial element in the development of our art as a family.

Some of these occasions stand out vividly in my memory. For instance there was that occasion in the hills of Orissa, when I stood among Sal trees with the sun behind me in the early morning, watching Peafowl; they had not spotted me because I was silhouetted against the sun. However, a troop of Black-faced Langurs, swinging in the trees overhead, certainly had seen me and with loud staccato barking warned one another of my presence. There was another time when I was on holiday in the Nilgiri Hills, south India. I was watching some wild elephants on a jungly mountainside, scratching themselves with foliage they had pulled down, when suddenly a pair of Fairy Bluebirds (*Irena puella*) flew into view with a fantastic flash of colour. Then there was an unforgettable morning a few years ago, when my father, my brother David and I were together on a mountain in the Eastern Highlands of Zimbabwe, watching a Verreaux's Eagle soaring high above us. Suddenly it folded its wings and plummeted in a dramatic dive down to the side of the mountain to catch some unsuspecting mammal. On a recent visit to that same country some friends and I were sitting in a boat in the Sanyati Gorge off Lake Kariba, while I was sketching a solitary bull elephant feeding near the water's edge. A troop of baboons had almost surrounded it and was exhausting its patience; so we went a little closer to have a better view of their antics. When only a few yards away the outboard motor stalled! The elephant angrily threatened us by flapping its ears, but fortunately the boatman got the outboard going again and with relief we moved quickly out of danger. I value those rough drawings done in such dramatic conditions.

The attitudes of birds and animals, though only maintained for a second or two, become imprinted on your mind with practice and experience. A quick drawing done on location with a few pencil strokes may not be an elegant picture but it represents a living creature's attitude as you saw it. The constant practice of making sketches from life imparts a skill and technique which eventually enables you to draw birds and animals from memory fairly accurately — and that is a useful asset.

You need time for this kind of activity; Nature cannot be studied in depth if you are in a hurry. I have found it necessary to go to distant places on occasions in order to observe certain birds and animals in their natural habitat, and to paint scenery and settings. For example, during one very cold spell in early January I went to the Scottish Highlands to study wildlife and to paint. No hotels or guest-houses were open at that time of year so I stayed in the Torridon Youth Hostel, from where I was able to make painting trips to nearby spots. Not far from Torridon village a scene caught my fancy: a splendid rocky outcrop near the road that runs beside the loch. Behind this rock were the scree slopes of the mighty Liathach. The freezing conditions and beginning of a blizzard presented a scene that I wanted to capture, so I turned the car just off the road and sat sketching with drawing-pad over the steering wheel, and pastels beside me on the passenger seat. I worked for an hour and a half, with sips of hot coffee from a flask, by which time I had virtually completed the picture, capturing the sombre colours amid the swirling flurries of snow — which were fortunately too intermittent to settle on the car windscreen and block the view. By then I was cold and the light had gone, so I returned to the Youth Hostel. Any touching up of the picture could

D.M. Henry. Zebra.

Bruce Henry. Red Deer Stag - drawn among a herd at Warnham Park, Sussex. Pencil. 1984.

be done at leisure on a later occasion.

In fact, little touching up was necessary (a fresh drawing done on location can easily be spoilt by over-embellishment); but two years later I returned to that picture and, with pastel pencils, drew in two Red Deer stags just where I had imagined them to be! Before actually drawing those stags, however, I had spent a day at Warnham Park in West Sussex, sketching Red Deer stags and hinds in a large herd. Some of those pencil sketches are illustrated on these pages and on page 46; the finished picture can be seen in Colour Plate 38.

In the world of wildlife art, settings are of the utmost importance. Backgrounds and foregrounds can make or break pictures, and any wildlife artist knows how much time he or she has to spend both studying settings and actually painting them. I have sometimes taken longer doing the setting in a picture than the actual creature which is being illustrated. Of course, if the artist is content to depict a bird on a twig with a plain white background, well and good; I have generally, however, preferred to give the bird more of a setting, and I know that my father and brother felt the same. As a result we have all spent a lot of time just painting settings. Whereas David was able to do this almost entirely in his studio, my father and I worked more on location.

George Henry was not a landscapist, although he did hundreds of landscapes in his time, some of them excellent; he never found it easy to paint background scenery for his birds and was much happier doing close settings with branches, foliage or rocks in the foreground. On one occasion he had done a drawing of a Ceylon Shahin Falcon which had just struck a Pompadour Green Pigeon in flight. Being unsure about a background for this he asked David to paint the background! The resulting joint effort is Plate IV in J.G. Mavrogordato's book, *A Falcon in the Field* (Knightly Vernon Ltd, 1966). Each part of the painting is typical of its painter.

On another occasion my father had painted, in tempera, a Ceylon Trogon sitting on a looped jungle vine. He never got beyond painting an over-all green background for its jungle setting, and the picture remained unfinished for several years. In his old age he felt unwilling to work on the picture and asked me to finish it — although I should mention that this was only after I had had the opportunity of watching a pair of Ceylon Trogons during a visit to Sri Lanka! I was able to study them for several minutes, perched and in flight in the forest, so there was ample time to observe their shape and behaviour. The picture was my father's concept, so anything done by me was rather cosmetic. I did some work on the Trogon itself (a male) and the vine on which it was resting, painted a forest setting with another tree or two, some bamboos and undergrowth, a little chink of blue sky showing at the top and a female bird flying away in the distance. The end result of our joint efforts is shown in Colour Plate 9.

Bruce Henry. Reclining Red Deer Stag. Warnham Park, Pencil. 1984

Bruce Henry. African Elephant. Drawn from life in Howell's Zoo Park

D.M. Henry. Study of Gyr Falcon. Pencil.

Despite my father's diffidence about landscape backgrounds, his skill in painting *settings* was tremendous. He painted on location in forest and hedgerow, on cliffs and mountains, on moors and estuaries. All this work was stock-in-trade for his later paintings and illustrations for books. For instance, many years ago he did an oil-painting of a pair of Ceylon Junglefowl, with the cock sitting resplendent on a raised branch-like root in the jungle. The setting was entirely appropriate. It was only after his death that I discovered another beautiful oil-painting of that same setting, done by him on location many years previously.

My brother David approached things differently. He would spend hours in the wild, watching birds and animals with his binoculars. He rarely took a sketch-book; instead, he was able to take in the 'feel' of the surroundings as well as much of their detail. He had a remarkable (some would call it photographic) memory for the world of Nature, so that when he returned home — or to camp — he would recall what he had seen and promptly draw a series of sketches of birds in various life-like attitudes; he would outline the head or tail in several positions on the one body and later choose which he preferred to use for a painting. Many examples of these pencil drawings are illustrated in this book. His observations of scenes and settings were so engraved on his mind that even years after the event he would be able to reproduce an authentic setting for a bird. He worked mainly in gouache, tempera and oils. He used cabinet-specimens of birds for close-up detail and measurements; and he brought foliage and flowers into his studio to paint close-up. Take any finished picture by David and it is safe to say that its setting breathes the very *ethos* of a scene in Nature which was clearly recorded in his memory.

My own methods are different again. In addition to binoculars I usually take the following items on Nature walks: spiral-backed sketch-book, soft pencil, eraser and penknife all in a khaki satchel. If a bird particularly attracts my interest I do a few quick

D.M. Henry. Study of Sparrowhawk. Pencil.

17. D.M. Henry. Ceylon Junglefowl. Gouache.

18. D.M. Henry. Nuthatch. Gouache.

19. *D.M. Henry. Red Bishop - studies. Gouache.*

20. D.M. Henry. Golden Eagle with Ptarmigan. Oil.

21. D.M. Henry. *White-faced Duck.* Gouache.

22. D.M. Henry. Gyrfalcon. Gouache/tempera. 1976(?).

23. *D.M. Henry. European Bee-eater. Gouache/tempera.*

24. D.M. Henry. Heuglin's Robin. Gouache/tempera.

D.M. Henry. Studies of Pygmy Kingfisher. Pencil.

D.M. Henry. White-faced Whistling Duck - field sketches. Pencil.

sketches of it before moving on, without shading or embellishment. If it sits long enough for me to pick out the shade on its anatomy I try to develop the sketch. Sometimes I carry a small box of water-colour paints in case I have the chance to make a quick study in colour. However, it must be said that on many occasions sketching on location is not possible, so one has to rely on memory and experience to make a few quick drawings at home. When doing a studio painting I have often made use of a little sketch drawn years previously. I really enjoy sketching from Nature — which is just as well, because I rely quite extensively on sketches done on site.

Bruce Henry. Red Fox - drawn from a captive animal. Pencil. 1981.

Nature is such a vast area of interest that I have been attracted to the painting of landscape as well as wildlife. The sight of a river estuary, lake or mountain scene has urged me for its intrinsic beauty to paint it. This I usually do in water-colour or in pastel. Both of these are reasonably quick mediums and I can often complete an on-location painting in two or three hours, depending on weather conditions.

In a later chapter I describe my painting techniques in greater detail; here it is sufficient to say that when working on location in water-colour I do not attempt a large painting, certainly nothing larger than 35 cm × 25 cm, and usually a little smaller. Smaller sizes of paper are easier to carry around and the paint dries quicker. For pastel work, however, larger paper is appropriate.

I find great fascination in the attempt to capture something of Nature's mystique and its moods. Moods — in Britain how appropriate that word is! Thanks to the changeable weather we enjoy, things do not always go according to plan. I was recently painting Beinn Alligin on a rather sombre day. I had left the car at the roadside a hundred yards away, made my way across heather and bog and set up my easel and water-colours. I had barely painted the mountains and a wash showing the cloud-filled sky, when it started to spot with rain. I lifted the picture and held it upside down while I quickly made my

Bruce Henry. Tame male Kestrel. Pencil. 1982.

way back to the car. When I looked at it inside the car the paint had run and given the effect of a rainstorm over Beinn Alligin. It's an ill wind that blows nobody any good! Fortunately, I was able to return to the site and complete the sketch after the rain had stopped.

Let me now revert to that initial question, How do you set about drawing birds and animals? Assuming that you have a basic knowledge of drawing and are a student of wildlife, the important thing is to be able, while watching the movement of a creature, to capture some aspect of this movement. It is comparatively easy to draw a bird quietly perched or an animal which is standing still — but in the wild few creatures want to sit still for long! It therefore takes practice to be able to sketch quick movements as if stopped by a camera, but the skill will come with perseverance.

It is useful to have some knowledge of a creature's anatomy; and it helps if you know roughly where its centre of gravity is when it sits or stands, so that you do not draw it as if it were off-balance! By way of example, let me return to the Red Deer scene. Imagine that I am watching a Red Deer stag among a herd. The animal's body is presenting a side view but its head is looking towards me. Unless it takes fright it will stand like that for a few seconds at least, and in this brief moment or two I have to assess the shape of its torso, the angle of head and neck and the curves of the antlers. I complete the body with three or four strokes; then add the head, neck and antlers, being careful to show any perspective if the head is slightly turned. By the time I am ready to draw the legs the animal has moved on several paces. I either have to draw in the legs as I saw them earlier, or else make a separate study of them in their new position. If the stag completely changes position I quickly start another sketch, perhaps on the next page. Soon I will be sketching another member of the herd. As far as possible I have to move with the herd from a discreet distance; they do not trust me, even though they have been watching me for an hour or so. Finally the

D.M. Henry. Red Fox.

Bruce Henry. Red Deer Stags, Warnham Park. Pencil. 1984.

herd moves off, and weariness drives me homewards. In this way some drawings get more or less finished while others remain for ever unfinished. No matter, several pages of drawings of living animals have added to the usefulness of the sketch-book.

It is not easy to draw birds in flight. When wings are flapping rapidly it is difficult to select any one angle of wing-slope, but with practice it is possible to isolate certain perspectives so that they look right in a drawing. If they don't look right, keep drawing the curves until they do! This may sound trite, but there is no short-cut other than resorting to copying photographs. If necessary let photographs help you, but your most fruitful and original work will be the result of watching Nature and sketching as you watch.

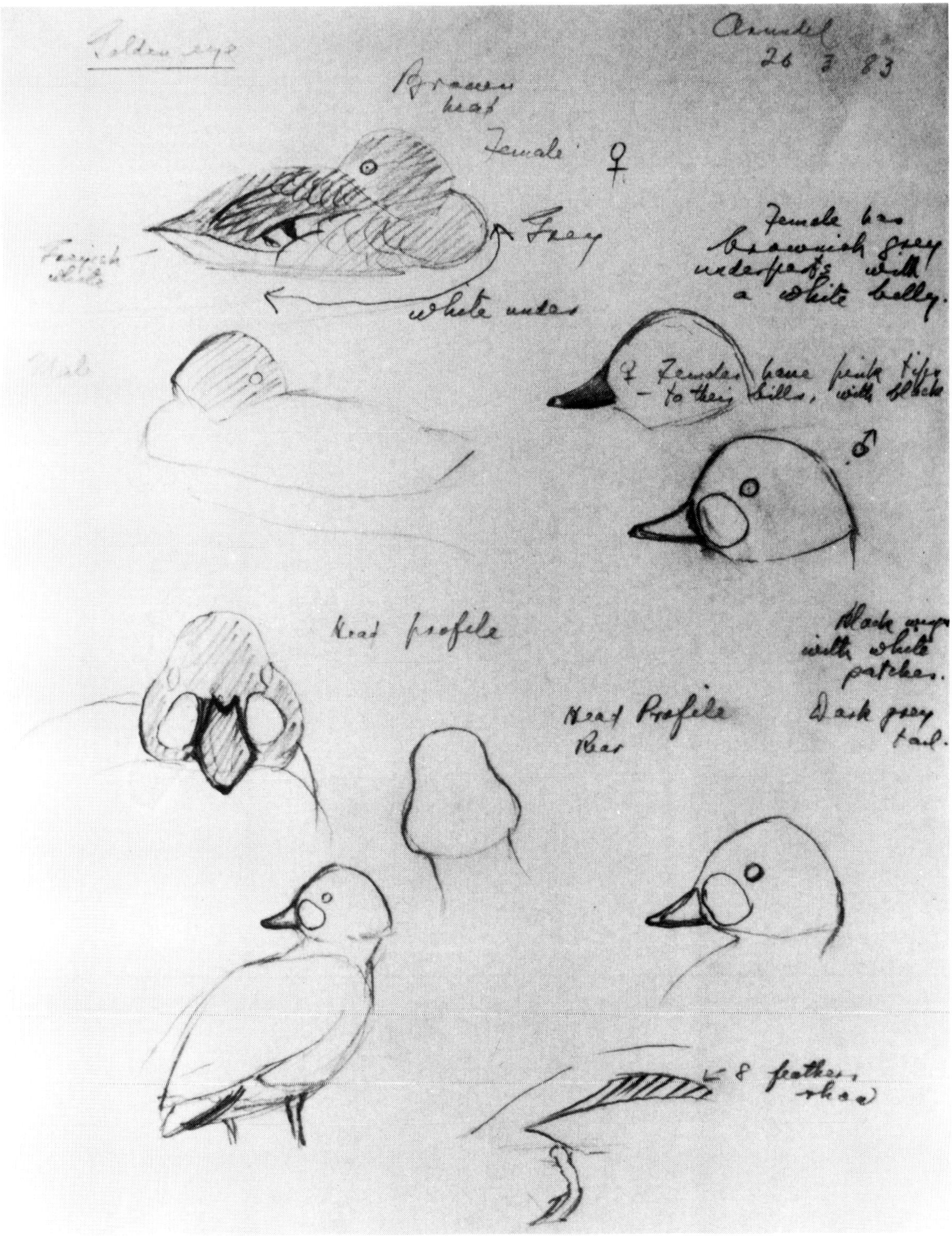

Bruce Henry. Goldeneye - sketches at Wildfowl Trust. Pencil. 1983.

D.M. Henry. Falcons in Flight - Merlin and Peregrine. Pencil.

One very useful way to do this is to sit in a hide at one of the RSPB or Wildfowl Trust reserves. These are visited by many wild species; and with binoculars, pad and pencil you can spend an hour or so producing lots of quick action-sketches of ducks and geese, gulls, terns and waders — a most enjoyable way of drawing from Nature in relative comfort.

As I stand drawing a flying bird I am holding a mental conversation with myself along these lines: 'This wing looks wrong in relation to the other, I've drawn it too rounded. Better have another go at that shape ... I'll draw the new shape over the old to save rubbing out ... There now, how does that look?' All this rumination goes on with frequent use of the binoculars, and perhaps a gap of several minutes before you see another flying bird in a similar attitude. Illustrations of this kind of drawing

G.M. Henry. Brahminy Kite. Pencil. 1943.

D.M. Henry. Flight Studies of Peregrine, Merlin, Hobby, Sparrowhawk, Cuckoo and Kestrel. Pencil.

G.M. Henry. Flight Studies of Black-shouldered Kite. Pen and ink. 1942.

can be seen on pages 64 and 96.

Let me now comment briefly on certain aids to wildlife art. First, the use of specimens. Cabinet skins of birds or stuffed specimens from museums can be helpful in supplying details and measurements. Even so it is likely that fleshy parts of the bird will have shrivelled, and feathers may have faded. In some cases, e.g. of very rare or extinct species, artists have little option but to rely on specimens. My brother David had to paint a Dodo as part of a stamp series for the Government of Mauritius. The bird had become extinct about 1680 and David was dependent on Savery's oil-painting of the Dodo at the British Museum (Natural History).

Dead birds or animals, brought in soon after death, are an extremely valuable source of information; their limbs have not shrivelled nor

Bruce Henry. Barn Owl - sketches made at the Hawk Conservancy, Weyhill. Pencil. 1981.

Bruce Henry. Turkestan Eagle Owl (the Hawk Conservancy, Weyhill). Pencil. 1980.

feathers faded. Useful studies of them, painted in colour and preferably life-size, can be made in studio conditions. We have made extensive use of such specimens, and examples are illustrated in Colour Plates 2 and 10. C.F. Tunnicliffe is well remembered for great work done in this field; and I imagine that many professional wildlife artists follow similar practice.

Game parks and zoos can be a useful source of material for painting, so long as it is remembered that captive animals usually look captive! I am personally indebted to such institutions, which I visit from time to time, particularly to draw large animals and birds of prey. Live creatures are better than dead ones, even if captive; and some of these private collections may be the only way of seeing certain species alive.

Finally, a word about the use of photographs. There is no doubt that nowadays much use is made of photographs in wildlife art, and this must encourage greater accuracy on the whole. I use photographs sometimes for the checking of detail and shape; but none of the Henry family has wanted to copy photographs, preferring the originality of sketches done from life or from memory. So long as photography assists wildlife art it can be helpful, but it can be no substitute for field studies. Every wildlife artist may decide on his or her techniques but will surely find Nature herself as the real source of inspiration.

CHAPTER 4

THE ARTISTS AT WORK

G.M. Henry. Studies of Spotted Eagle Owl (Africa).

Our family's kind of art has been representational, for we have always attempted to portray what we saw or remembered, both in landscape and in wildlife. At the same time we have been at liberty to modify what we saw, in the interests of composition. When painting a landscape, for example, we are aiming to produce a *picture*, and if it would enhance the composition to alter the position of, say, a tree or rock, then we do so — particularly as such objects may be quite incidental to the picture as a whole.

We also select from Nature what we want. In sketching a Robin, for instance, we may find ourselves drawing it in numerous attitudes, with just a few strokes sufficient to convey the posture. The bird may be bathing, preening, scratching or yawning; and, while these quick sketches are fun to do and useful to have in a sketch-book they would not necessarily contribute to a desirable picture. Therefore one tends to select attitudes which appear more pictorially attractive. The danger of this is that it can lead to a conventional style of painting. Doubtless all of us have been slaves of convention many a time, perhaps most of the time, but I must confess that I would not want framed pictures of soggy robins or mating elephants . . .

Our individual styles have much in common. Each of us has done some paintings which might have been the work of one of the others. An example of this is the Trogon picture (Colour Plate 9). It would have been out of the question for me to complete my father's painting had our styles been grossly disparate. Unquestionably, each of us has learned from the others in numerous ways, and David and I naturally owe our father the biggest debt of all. Nevertheless, on closer examination a considerable variety of style is apparent. It will be left to Donald Watson, in Chapter 6, to assess our work; so I will limit myself to describing how each of us has developed his own way of doing things.

I begin with my father, George Henry. From his youth he was interested in the close-up drawing of insects and birds. In Chapter 2 I have described his work as a draughtsman in marine biology when he was required to draw specimens from microscopic observation. In those days there was no colour photography, so all detailed illustrations of specimens had to be hand-painted. Examples of my father's paintings, viewed as through a microscope, can be seen in Colour Plate 3. In life, the Salticid Spider (Colour Plate 8) is less than the size of a little finger-nail! Not surprisingly, he approached his bird-painting with a similar emphasis on accurate, detailed representation, and for many years produced material in great detail. Throughout half a century he made measured drawings and paintings of birds, done from freshly dead specimens, and they were kept in his portfolios as works of reference. Most of them proved invaluable for subsequent paintings and illustrations. Examples of these studies can be seen on pages 86 and 99 and in Colour Plate 10. Observe the detail in the study of a *Ceylon Highland Nightjar* (*Caprimulgus indicus kelaarti*), shown on page 56; and the interesting attitudes of a Wood Pigeon's feet, on page 57. The flying Black-headed Oriole (*Oriolus xanthornus ceylonensis*), shown in Colour Plate 2, was painted from a fresh specimen with its wings and tail pinned out on a board. My father produced a huge number of these colour-studies and pencil drawings.

However, he began to feel a sense of dissatisfaction with over-detailed work, specially when he was no longer working from a microscope; and much of his later work shows only a suggestion of detail. In style and artistic outlook he was influenced by some great wildlife artists of the past, notably Fuertes, Thorburn and Lodge. He looked back critically on some of his earlier work, particularly his *Coloured Plates of the Birds of Ceylon* (4 vols., Ceylon Government, Colombo, 1927-1935). Here is an extract from his memoirs:

> The painting of the plates suffered both in quantity and quality from several circumstances. In the first place I was expected to do them as a

D.M. Henry. Study of a Pheasant's Head.

spare-time occupation owing to Government regulations regarding the earning of fees over one's substantive salary. (Incidentally, the fees paid by Dr Wood, though very welcome at the time were, with hindsight, rather ludicrously inadequate — about £2.6s per plate!) This meant that bird-painting had to be relegated to periods of leave, public holidays etc. This seriously curtailed output, as bird-painting had to take its place among many other claimants for spare-time activities. A more important handicap, however, was my faulty technique, due to a false notion that 'pure water-colour', applied to white paper was the only legitimate medium for use in such a project. Pure, transparent water-colour, ideal as it is for some forms of art (notably landscape) is, in my opinion, utterly unsuitable for the detailed, close-up portrayal of birds; and attempting to use

G.M. Henry. Ceylon Highland Nightjar (Caprimulgus indicus kelaarti). Gouache.

25. D.M. Henry. Lanner Falcon. Gouache. 1971.

26. D.M Henry. Sable Antelope. Gouache/tempera. 1971.

27. Bruce Henry in his studio.

28. Bruce Henry. Sparrowhawks and Chicks. Watercolour. 1983.

29. *Bruce Henry. 'Fun on the Lek' - Black Game on Langdon Fell, Co. Durham. Watercolour. 1984.*

30. Bruce Henry. Peregrine Tiercel. Gouache. 1980.

31. Bruce Henry. Goldeneyes at Loch Leven. Watercolour. 1983.

32. Bruce Henry. Great Spotted Woodpeckers. Gouache. 1982.

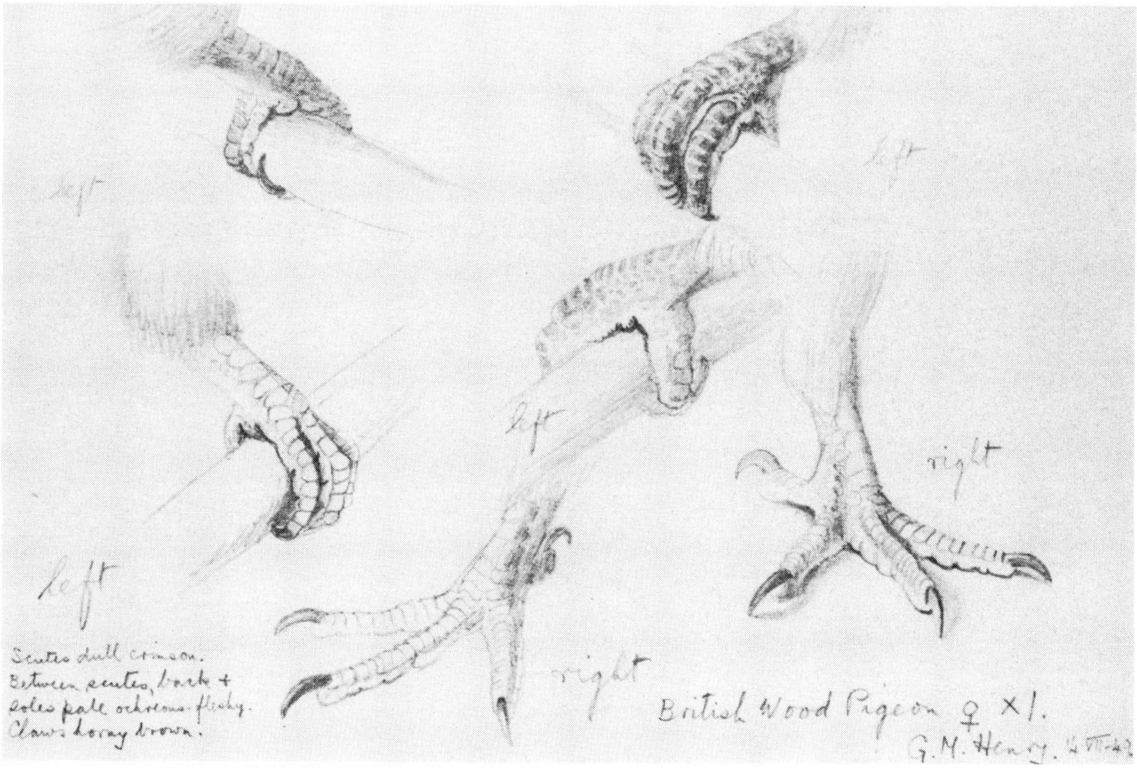

G.M. Henry. Studies of a Wood Pigeon's Feet. Pencil. 1949.

it for my purpose led to much wasted effort and frustration and the production of some very poor results. Had I but known of the virtues of gouache (opaque water-colour) or, better, egg-tempera used on toned paper, how very much more satisfactory in quality and output would the *Coloured Plates of the Birds of Ceylon* have been!

However, it is but fair to say that, at that period in Ceylon, artists' materials were very limited in variety and quality, and water-colour paints were all I could obtain. Suitable paper for painting on was also hard to get and, owing to the humid climate, was often foxed and ruined even before one bought it . . .

My father's difficulty in obtaining good art paper prompts a comment. He became so used to making do, that he habitually used odd scraps of paper for his field sketches. Sometimes he would take a lined notebook on his birding jaunts, and in this he would do his sketches — occasionally even in water-colour. He was reluctant to spend money on quality paper when he had 'perfectly good paper' at home, forgetting that this might have been in drawers for years! When I talked about the merits of acid-free paper and art board, I guessed he was saying to himself, 'Well, the old masters didn't have these fancy products ... ' However, though some of his earlier work has suffered from the effects of long years in the tropics, most of the later work is in excellent condition.

Some of my father's comments about pure water-colour techniques may be debatable, but at least they explain his preference for gouache and tempera, and it was in these mediums that his best work was done. He had a daily egg for breakfast, so there were always eggs in the fridge. He would take a little yoke from a fresh egg, dilute it considerably with water and use this as his medium. (Incidentally, not even the shells were wasted; he would draw portraits of television personalities on them as he watched the programmes , and then range them in egg-boxes in a quaint sort of rogues' gallery!) Occasionally he painted in oils and I have a number of oil-painted landscapes which he did on location in Sri Lanka. It is remarkable that he was able to work in this medium for so many hours on end in the hot, humid conditions of that island; but he was used to it, having lived most of his life there. On my recent visit to Sri Lanka, the most that I could manage on location was about two hours at a stretch. Latterly, my father did comparatively few oil-paintings, preferring to concentrate on tempera; and his enthusiasm for it was such that he often tried to persuade me to adopt the medium. I always listened courteously but kept my options open!

Now some remarks about my own way of working. I paint in water-colour, pastel and oil, roughly in that order of preference. I enjoy painting in oil but not the palaver of setting it all up and cleaning up afterwards! Moreover, it takes me a lot longer to do an oil-painting than to do one of similar size and subject in water-colour or pastel; consequently my

Bruce. Henry. Green Woodpeckers. Pastel. 1984.

attempts are reserved for somewhat rare moments of inspiration. Of course, working in pastel is also very messy and, in the studio, dusty; but I love the medium and enjoy its qualities. After a period of working in water-colour, perhaps depicting some creature in detail, I know of no better release from the thraldom of detail than to take a stick of pastel, sideways on, and apply it with gusto to a large sheet of textured, tinted paper! Pastel gives me a great sense of boldness and freedom, and I like its rugged qualities as well as its delicate hues; I also enjoy going home with a more-or-less finished picture after a couple of hours' work on location.

As in other mediums, I have never felt bound to any convention about pastel techniques. I study the methods of other pastel painters and try out their suggestions, but have developed my own technique. In the next chapter I describe in detail how I painted *Beeches and Magpies at Arundel* (Colour Plate 39). There are three pastel paintings shown in this book (Colour Plates 38–40), and I hope they illustrate something of my style. Two were painted in Britain and one in Australia; all were painted on location, except for the birds and animals. The scenes represent what I saw as I painted, apart from a few minor items added or left out for the sake of composition. The Magpies and deer were drawn in the studio, from memory or with the help of my field sketches.

Skies always fascinate me, and I try various ways of painting them. In pastel I usually cover the sky area with white chalk (or any other basic colour required at the time of painting), which I then rub in with my finger until it is smooth and of consistent density. This becomes the base on to which I can add, say, pale cobalt, French ultramarine or other appropriate colours — which I rub in, mixing with the white, giving a smooth effect. I then chalk in the clouds with their highlights and shadows, boldly applying the pastel with side-on strokes, sweeps and curves. For this purpose I prefer to use short pieces of pastel. Clouds are full of colour even when they are dark and sombre, so I try to capture something

Bruce Henry. Woodbury Down, near Exeter. Water-colour. 1981.

of their variety. Here again, composition is important. I 'arrange' the clouds to make an appealing composition. Nature will have given me the general idea and the colour scheme; I as an artist am free to modify what Nature displays.

Pure water-colour, as with pastel, calls for boldness — but also considerable speed in application. There are skills in knowing when to use your paper wet and when to use it dry, and what effects can be achieved when it is neither wet nor dry, but just damp enough. This medium challenges and, at the same time, tantalises me. It is not an easy medium and does not allow much room for mistakes. Rarely do I feel more daunted than when I sit before a sheet of clean, white art paper which awaits my water-colours! Nevertheless it is a delightful medium which I enjoy using. There is a freshness and simplicity about good water-colour paintings which is appealing.

Most of my water-colour paintings begin with a wash background, often laid on wet or damp paper. When this is thoroughly dry I re-wet the surface and

Bruce Henry. By South Farm Lane, Budleigh Salterton, Devon. Water-colour. 1981.

paint in, with blobs and streaks, the colours I want. When dry, this leaves an indefinite effect rather like the out-of-focus background in a photograph. Examples of this can be seen in Colour Plates 28 and 32. On to the wash-base can be added more definite features, as in *Goldeneyes at Loch Leven* (Colour Plate 31). In this example, the islands on the loch and the hill in the distance are in relatively sharp focus. The Goldeneyes, and the grasses in the foreground were the last items to be painted. The pictures in Colour Plates 28, 29 and 34 were also painted in pure water-colour.

I agree with my father about the difficulty of depicting minute detail in pure water-colour; so, if necessary, I do not hesitate to paint detailed subjects in gouache. For example, the Great Spotted

Woodpeckers and the dead tree, shown in Colour Plate 32, were painted in gouache on a pure water-colour background. The same applies to *Small Tortoiseshell on Buddleia* (Colour Plate 37), where the butterfly, flowers and some of the foliage were painted in gouache, the rest in pure water-colour. Obviously, the larger a picture is, the easier it is to paint detail. If a small picture demands fine detail, I prefer to paint it in gouache. There is nothing *infra dig* about the use of gouache, it is simply much easier to use!

Many of my scenic backgrounds for wildlife paintings are based on water-colour or pastel studies done on location. In a few instances, as in the case of *Red Deer on the Slopes of Liathach* (Colour Plate 38), I have added animals to a painting which was done on location. The same procedure was used for *Beeches and Magpies at Arundel* (Colour Plate 39). When I paint close-up studies of birds, I bring foliage into the studio and prop it up in front of me. This is how I painted the ivy in the picture in Colour Plate 35. The original idea for this came when I saw some trailing fronds of ivy hanging down a bank in Devon. The light and shade on the sandy bank appealed to me and I decided to paint a Wren in that kind of setting. *Fun on the Lek* (Colour Plate 29) is a large water-colour work which I painted after I had been studying Black Grouse on a lek in County Durham. I watched the birds for two days, so there was ample time not only to sketch their antics (see page 64) but also to make a quick water-colour study of the scene, showing the mid-morning colours of that April day.

Water-colour painting poses problems in extreme climates. In hot, desert conditions the paint dries almost immediately and the paper does not stay damp long enough to achieve a smooth wash; and in extremely cold conditions the water turns into ice! Stupidly, I took some water-colour paint to Amberley Wild Brooks in Sussex, intending to make a study on a cold, frosty day. Two or three inches of snow covered the ground, and the flooded fields were frozen. I placed the paint-box and water-

Bruce. Henry. Field sketches of Black Grouse on Lek. Pencil. 1984.

container on a fence and started to paint. All went well for a minute or so. Then the wet paint froze on the paper and soon even the brush froze! The paint only thawed when I was on my way home in the car, causing horrid trickles of colour down the paper. Of course, I should have taken pastels, not water-colours. It is so easy to be wise after the event ...

On a visit to the Scottish Highlands, 700 miles from home, I planned to make studies of snow on the mountains (I have already mentioned this occasion, in Chapter 3). A friend said, 'Wouldn't you find it far simpler to take a series of photos up there?' My answer was: 'Yes, of course, and I probably will take photos; but I can achieve more through painting than by photography.' Doubtless he thought I was crazy, in view of the weather conditions at the time. I must confess that I found the intense cold on the mountains almost unbearable, but went ahead with my plan and made a number of pastel studies of snow, grasses, rocks, frozen streams and light and shade on the slopes. I also took some photos. When I saw these back at home and compared them with the pastel studies it was quite clear that the pastels had captured the colours more accurately than the photos.

I come now to the work of my brother David which, in many respects, eclipsed that of my father and me. He was a man of many parts, and his professional activities had to compete with falconry, in which he had a great interest. There is no doubt that his falconry enhanced his ability as a painter of raptors. However, any serious falconer knows how much time is involved in the training of hawks and falcons. The birds are a constant tie, demanding to be fed, weighed, flown and meticulously looked after. Whenever David went anywhere distant, he had to take his menagerie of falcons and hawks with him in his van. On one occasion when he visited us, he set up his huge African Crowned Eagle ('Tiara') just beyond the foot of the bed in our front bedroom, and had a Merlin on a block by the bedside. Carpets and wallpaper were suitably protected by newspaper! In the garden he had a

Peregrine on a block, and another falcon in the van — and ours was only one of many homes he visited. We used to wonder how he found time to paint!

When the family's bread and butter were getting low, falconry could not bring in the supplies and there were hard times for them all. Apart from raptors and other pets in their garden, David had one or two birds in cages in the house — sometimes out of cages! He had equipment lying here and there, tobacco-tins and pipes on shelves and tables. He used the lids of tobacco-tins as his pallettes, which he threw away when they were of no more use. During the Woodford years he was often nocturnal, painting well into the night with the aid of powerful lamps. Sometimes, however, he just did not feel like painting — and artists know the feeling! To quote Eric Hosking:

> . . . he had a typical artist's temperament, and if he was not in the mood for painting nothing would make him do so. (*British Birds* 70; 540, December 1977)

Detail was very important to David. His eyesight was such that he could paint remarkably minute detail, specially in plumage. Every whisker round a bird's beak was significant, and every feather a candidate for his picture. As a keen observer of living birds and animals, his knowledge of their anatomy and behaviour enabled him, with consummate skill, to record these features accurately in his paintings. His creatures always looked alive.

This insistence on detail affected not only the birds and animals but the backgrounds as well. For example, if you take your eye off a bird and look at its environment, you see that environment in focus; even if you look at the *distant* landscape, you see it in focus, though with some loss of detail. For this reason, no doubt, David felt it desirable to paint most of his pictures in clear detail. And he knew that there was a market for such work; he loved doing it, and there are many to admire it. Almost all the

D.M. Henry. Studies of Peregrine Falcon.

coloured plates of David's work in this book are examples of his fine detail. The head-and-shoulder painting of the *African Crowned Eagle*, shown in Colour Plate 15, is a very good example of his style. I quote Eric Hosking again:

> He was so good at painting landscapes, even including microscopic detail of moss and lichen on the rocks ... (*British Birds* 70: 541, December 1977)

David's main mediums were gouache, tempera and oils. He avoided pure water-colours, preferring the greater protential for detail afforded by opaque colours. His illustrations for books were done in gouache or tempera, as also many of his paintings for exhibitions. Nevertheless some of his greatest works were oil-paintings. The majority of these were much larger than his gouache pictures, but even in his smaller oil-paintings there is a remarkable degree of detail — and fine detail is not easy to paint in oils.

I have always admired David's skill with a pencil. He often drew his birds in detail, shading and all, before using their outlines for a painting. In this way he could establish the direction of light and the tones for his picture. A fine example of his pencil work is the unfinished drawing of a Peregrine, shown on page 67. As mentioned earlier, he was able to make good use of his own falcons, hawks and eagles, spending many hours sketching them. His knowledge of raptors is quite evident in every painting he did of them.

However, David had many irons in the fire, as we have seen, and it is hard to avoid the conclusion that his concentration suffered as a result of the time devoted to other activities. Here is an extract from a letter he wrote in July 1976:

> I am still very busy, but feeling terribly stale and most of my work showing signs of *ennui*.

Another comment appears in a letter written in the same year:

D.M. Henry. Unfinished study of Peregrine Falcon. Pencil.

> Am now struggling with Gyr for X's picture, background of which you know. Perspective won't come right, so am retiring *pro tem* from battle to consider. So far I've done ten drawings as experimentals.

Before finishing one picture David would often start another, and in this way have several paintings on the go. Inevitably, there were various half-finished works lying around the studio. In fact, after his death there were sufficient of his unfinished works to mount an exhibition. He was a perfectionist, and if he was not satisfied with some aspect of a painting he would stop work and take stock. If he could make the necessary alteration without spoiling the picture, he would do so; if not, the painting was laid aside until a better idea was forthcoming! However, when one considers the enormous volume of his output over the years, it is hardly surprising that some material never got finished.

I find, personally, that concentration comes and goes like the ebb and flow of a tide. Perhaps it has to be like that. No-one can maintain concentration for too long at a stretch, and artists as much as anyone need diversions to give themselves a break. Sometimes, even interruptions can provide a break if they don't come at the wrong time — it can cause problems if someone calls while you are laying a wash! The Henrys have all been family men with homes, wives and children, and our work has been carried on from the home-base and in the context of the family.

CHAPTER 5

THE MAKING OF A PICTURE

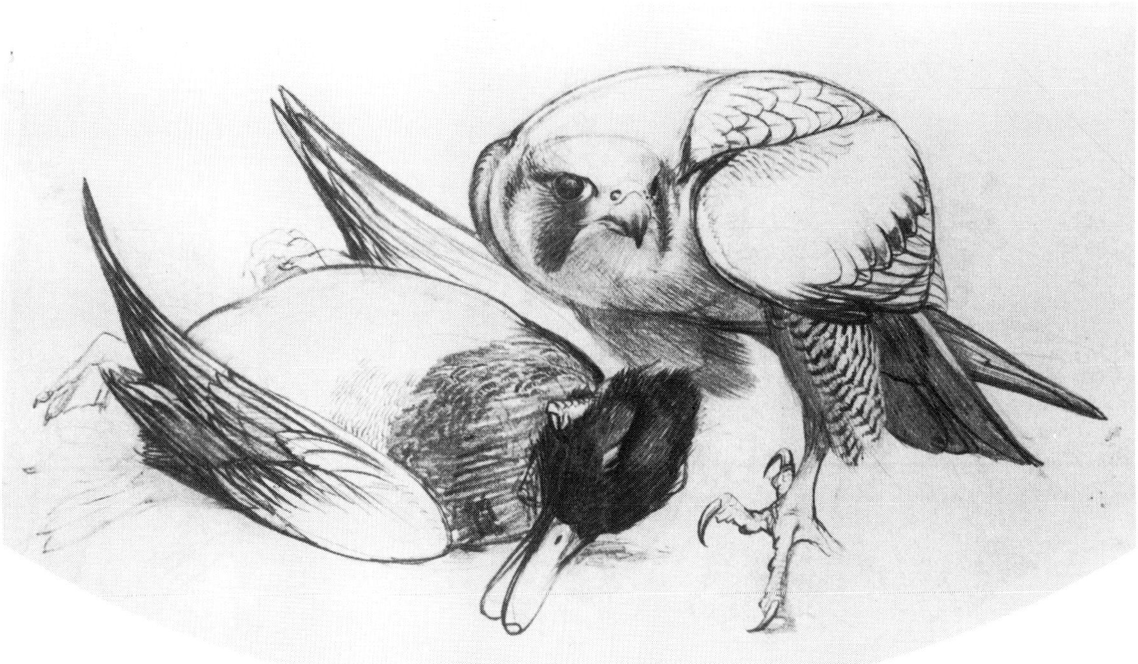

D.M. Henry. Sketch of Peregrine and Mallard.

In this chapter I describe how three of my paintings came about. Two are in water-colour and one in pastel.

(1) *Sparrowhawks and Chicks* (Water-colour, 585 mm × 381 mm). See illustrations on page 73 and in Colour Plate 28.

This painting owes its existence to an earlier, commissioned painting of a female Sparrowhawk at its nest (illustrated on the jacket). While painting the latter I decided to do a larger, more comprehensive work on a similar theme, showing a dead bird in one of the hawks' claws. Killing and eating smaller birds is what Sparrowhawks are all about, so I was keen to show a drama at the nest.

Before starting the picture some preliminary work was necessary. I visited a clump of old Scots Pines where I spent a couple of hours doing pencil sketches of their trunks and branches, and close-up studies of the bark. Moving on to a nearby spinney with younger pine trees I made a water-colour study of the setting so as to record suitable colours for a background in my picture. Aided by these sketches, I made a rough charcoal drawing of the Sparrowhawk family at their nest, in order to establish the general composition. The charcoal outlines were drawn and re-drawn several times with a few quick strokes. I then did a pencil drawing of the birds on separate paper, cut it out so as to include only the birds and attached it with 'Blutack' to the charcoal drawing. I changed its position several times until I was satisfied with the composition.

It was now time to start the detailed drawing of the subject. Using a sheet of layout paper I drew the birds from memory, aided by pencil and water-colour sketches done in the past. I also had cabinet skins of male and female Sparrowhawks, borrowed from a museum to give me accurate details and measurements. Many drawings were made before I selected the attitudes I wanted, and this took about two days. I decided that the nearest hawk should be

33. *Bruce Henry. Primrose and Ground Ivy. Gouache. 1982.*

34. Bruce Henry. 'Uneven Odds' - Golden Eagle and Mountain Hare. Watercolour. 1985.

35. Bruce Henry. Wren. Watercolour. 1981.

36. Bruce Henry. 'Liathach from Loch Clair'. Watercolour. 1984.

37. Bruce Henry. Small Tortoiseshell on Buddleia. Gouache. 1981.

38. Bruce Henry. *Red Deer on the slopes of Liathach.* Pastel. 1982-84.

39. Bruce Henry. Beeches and Magpies at Arundel. Pastel. 1981.

40. Bruce Henry. 'The Three Sisters', Katoomba, N.S.W., Australia. Pastel. 1984.

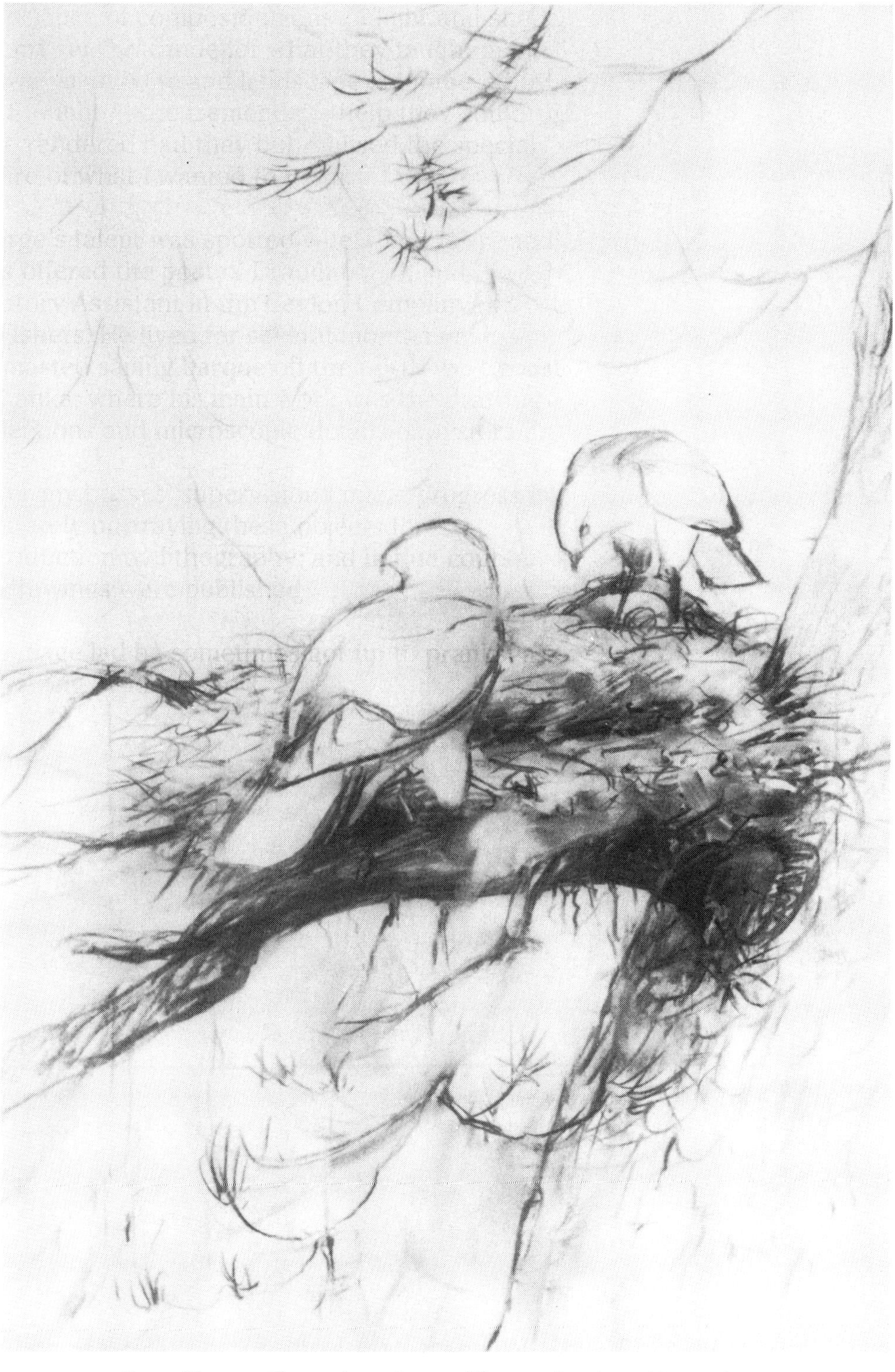

Bruce Henry. Charcoal mock-up of Sparrowhawks at Nest. 1983.

the female, and that it should have a dead Song Thrush in its claws. (The male would have brought the Thrush to the nest having killed and partly plucked it at a nearby plucking post.) I drew the Thrush, using a dead bird I found in a country lane; it had been killed by a passing car and was not too badly damaged to act as a model for my picture. Lastly I drew the trees and the nest. I then looked at the whole drawing in a mirror to check the proportions and shapes — you can often get a better idea of your picture by looking at it the wrong way round!

Selecting a sheet of Saunders 90 lb hot-press water-colour art paper, slightly larger than required for the painting, I stretched it on a drawing-board. This was done by thoroughly soaking the paper, placing it on the board and applying gum-strip round the edges. When the paper had thoroughly dried it was stretched, taut and ready for the drawing to be traced on to it. Next, I took the paper with the drawing on it, rubbed soft pencil all over the back of the paper, placed it on top of the stretched art paper and traced carefully over my drawing — feathers, markings and all. This left a clear, pencil impression on the art paper. It was now ready for the application of the water-colour paint.

To ensure the whiteness of the chicks and a few light areas on the hawks, I applied masking fluid to these areas and waited a couple of minutes for it to dry. In the meantime I prepared small pots of paint in various colours, and in sufficient quantity for the background of the picture. It was now time to wet the surface of the paper, using a soft decorator's brush and keeping the drawing-board horizontal. With a large sable brush I dipped into the pots of paint and quickly applied blues, greens, yellows and browns, blobbing and stippling the colours on the wet paper and allowing the paint to run. I added stronger colours where necessary. All this had to be done within a few minutes— once the paper had begun to dry it had to be left. When it had dried, an out-of-focus effect had been achieved for the general background.

Next I re-wet the surface of the paper with a fine mist spray from a spray-gun, and allowed it to dry off a little so that paint would not run too much. With the paper still horizontal I used a small sable brush, not too wet, to paint the young pine trunks in the background and the little branches protruding from them. Those trees were intentionally out of focus, but less so than the general background. While the paper was still damp I painted the foliage above the birds. One or two effects were added when the paper was dry.

The main tree trunk and branch were the next to be dealt with. I painted them a light red-brown initially, adding greens, crimson and darker brown to the wet paint. When it was dry I painted the markings of the bark and, with a damp brush, lifted a little paint here and there to show the highlights on the bark. I then worked on the nest, painting in the shadows so that the sticks stood out. Again, using a damp, flat-edged brush, I lifted out paint to show the prominent sticks to the right of the female Sparrowhawk, adding darker colouring on their shaded side. Next appeared the branches and the foliage in the foreground, including the young pine cones. Last of all I came to the birds. I removed the dry masking fluid with a soft eraser, exposing the white paper underneath. Then I painted the birds, light colours followed by dark, occasionally lifting out paint to show highlights. The Song Thrush took almost as long to paint as the Sparrowhawks; and the whole painting took three weeks to complete.

(2) *Liathach from Loch Clair* (Water-colour, 330 mm × 515 mm). See Colour Plate 36.

A small sketch done on location was the basis for this picture. I had re-visited Glen Torridon — that wilderness whose grandeur and rugged beauty never fail to attract me. I set up my easel on the edge of Loch Clair at a point where there was a particularly good view of Liathach, showing part of the loch. I attached a small paint-box and a sheet of thick art paper, size 175 mm × 240 mm, on to a piece of hardboard and clamped this in a horizontal position on the easel. The water was in a small non-spill container attached to the paint-box. In the painting I showed snow-capped Liathach with its summit partly covered by cloud, the lower ascent of Beinn Eighe to the right, part of Loch Clair, the braes and Scots Pines across the water and the grass growing out of the shallows of the loch. I stood while painting, and the work took two hours.

Subsequently, I painted a larger version of that scene, in my studio. I placed a sheet of tracing paper over the smaller painting and ruled it into 2 cm squares covering the whole picture area. Then, taking a large sheet of layout paper, I marked out 4 cm squares on it and made a drawing of the scene, correctly proportioned, four times the size of the smaller picture. I traced this drawing on to a sheet of Saunders 90 lb 'NOT' water-colour art paper which I had previously stretched on a large drawing-board. I felt that the picture would need some living creatures to enhance it, so I drew three sheep on the nearer bank across the loch. To do this I first made several drawings of sheep on separate paper; from these I selected three, and placed cut-outs of them on the art paper in various positions to determine where they would fit best. When satisfied I traced them on to the art paper, and was now ready to commence painting.

I prepared a selection of water-colours in the shades and quantities I might need. Then, tilting the drawing-board towards me, I laid a pale blue-grey wash right down the paper, using a large sable brush. When the paper was thoroughly dry I applied masking fluid with a fine brush on all the snowy areas and the sheep, and allowed it to dry. I then changed the drawing-board to the horizontal position and painted the blue of Liathach, allowing it to fade into the mist on the left side; then the different hues of the slope of Beinn Eighe, merging them into the lower slopes of Liathach. While the paint was wet I added warmer colours (e.g. yellows and purples) on the nearer slopes, diluting the paint as I came down to the level of the loch. The blue on the top of Liathach was still damp enough for me to dab out paint with a dry handkerchief so as to create the light clouds near the summit. All this work had to be done quickly; and then the paper was allowed to dry.

It was now time to paint the clouds. Re-wetting the paper down to the level of the loch, I applied varying mixtures of French ultramarine and burnt sienna to the sky, dabbing out paint or adding a little more blue as necessary. Again, this had to be done quickly while the paper was wet. When I had achieved the effect I wanted, the paper was left to dry. Next I rubbed off the dried masking fluid from the mountains, exposing the snowy areas. They were of course not pure white but pale blue, having received the first wash. I touched in the rocks and shadows on Liathach with a small brush charged with pale ultramarine. As the main areas of sky and mountains were now completed, I was ready to proceed with the nearer landscape.

Lightly wetting the lower half of the picture I painted the grasses in the loch — the damp paper gave them a slightly out-of-focus effect. When the paper had dried I applied light yellow ochre to the banks and braes beyond the loch and, with the paint still wet, I painted in some red-browns to give the effect of dry bushes. When the paper was again quite dry, I re-wet the loch only and painted the dark grey reflections in the still water and the ripples in the left foreground. Once again the paper was left to dry, and then I used some darker browns to give sharper edges to the banks, and to show the dry heather in the foreground. I added some green on the bank near the sheep, and then painted the lighter-coloured trees, leaving out patches on their trunks. These patches were made even lighter by lifting out earlier paint with a stiff, damp brush. The bracken and grass stalks in the foreground were created in the same way. I then painted the Scots Pines, first the trunks and branches, then the foliage; also the small plantation of pine trees in the middle distance.

Finally, the sheep. I rubbed off the masking fluid

and painted their heads and feet, and the shadows. A few finishing touches, including my signature, completed the picture.

(3) *Beeches and Magpies at Arundel* (Pastel, 267 mm × 368 mm). See Colour Plate 39.

On a sunny Saturday morning in October I set up my easel at Swanbourne Lake, Arundel, Sussex by the footpath which skirts the lake. I had a sheet of grey Ingres-Fabriano paper ready, backed with a sheet of newspaper and attached to hardboard with two large rubber bands. The board was then clamped to the easel in an upright position, and my boxes of pastels were placed on a folding stool at my side. I laid a large plastic sheet under the easel to catch fallen pieces of pastel.

Having decided which part of the landscape to include in the picture, I used a piece of grey pastel — a lighter grey than the paper — to outline the main features of the scene. This took several minutes, after which I pastelled the small area of sky and its reflection in the lake with soft white pastel, rubbing it with my finger to give an even tone. Next, I applied cobalt blue, rubbing it over the white and adding more cobalt where necessary, so achieving a smooth, blue-white effect. I then pastelled the basic colours of the wooded hills, the reeds and path, adding light or dark colours to give detail and depth to the background. I did the reflections with downward strokes to make them look watery. Next came the lighter reeds with their shadows, the golden colours in the foreground and the blobs of sunlight on the path.

I was now ready to pastel in the trees, adding the highlit tones on the trunks and the shadows cast by the branches. I pastelled the larger branches, with their light and shade, followed by the smaller ones. To achieve the sharper strokes necessary for trailing branches I used the end-edge of the pastel after first rubbing it on a piece of fine sand-paper to obtain a sharper edge. Finally, I added tufts and grasses where relevant, and the golden leaves on the beeches. Interested passers-by had caused a little delay, but the work was completed in a morning.

Back in the studio I set about drawing the Magpies. I made a number of little drawings, from which I selected three. I carefully cut them out and, with forceps, lightly placed them on the picture, changing their positions until I was satisfied with the composition. The next task was to remove the pastel from under these cut-outs. I did this by placing each of the Magpie stencils over their respective positions and brushing out the pastel from those areas. I then had three small Magpie shapes on the picture. It only remained for me to draw in the Magpies with sharp-tipped pastel pencils (of the kind produced by Conté, and Schwan-Stabilo). The work on the Magpies took as long as the rest of the picture!

I did not spray-fix the picture, because that would have altered its tone and texture. Instead, I stuck the picture on acid-free cardboard (using acid-free paste) and left it to dry overnight between weighted boards. The moisture from the paste had permeated the paper from behind, and so helped to fix the pastel. When the picture was thoroughly dry I tapped its edge on to a hard surface to dislodge any pastel dust. I normally take my paintings to a professional picture-framer, but not in the case of pastels as these are particularly vulnerable until safely behind glass. I therefore ordered the mount and frame and put the picture in myself. The mount served a double purpose: it enhanced the picture, and also kept it from impinging on the glass.

Every picture tells a story ... Never was this more true for me than when I did a painting of a Peregrine. The picture is illustrated in Colour Plate 30. After laying a water-colour wash for the background, I painted the rest of the picture in gouache. Now for the story!

On a frosty day in early January I went to the Hawk Conservancy at Weyhill — open to the public and an excellent centre for raptors of many species — where I spent several hours sketching a Peregrine

D.M. Henry. European Kestrel.

sitting on a block. The bird allowed me close enough to make detailed studies of its plumage as it sat preening and viewing its surroundings. Back home, I made several more drawings of the Peregrine, using the sketches from that visit. However, although I chose one of those drawings for the planned picture, I was unable to make headway because I lacked the inspiration for a suitable setting. I wanted the bird to be sitting on a cliff rock with the sea in the background; and although I had pencil sketches of mountain rocks, they were unsuitable for a sea-cliff scene. So, late one morning, I decided to drive to the north Cornish coast, 200 miles away, to sketch cliff rocks. My wife nobly rustled up a quick lunch and we were off for two or three days! With this fresh material I was able to proceed with the picture, which involved about a week's work.

Bruce Henry. Tiger, drawn in Paignton Zoo.

As soon as I hear Chiffchaffs and Willow Warblers in the Spring, and see the wild-flowers coming on, I want to go off to the woods and hedgerows to sketch; so at this time of year I spend many a day in the fresh air with water-colours or pastels, painting Primroses, Violets, Anemones and such like. I usually take a flask of hot coffee and some sandwiches — and a camera. If a picture has to be finished at home because rain stopped work it is useful to have a photo to assist with detail.

Climate can be an awkward factor to reckon with. I am quite used to working out of doors in cold conditions, with mitts on my hands if necessary; but in tropical countries there are other problems. For instance, I was doing a water-colour study of the Victoria Falls in Zimbabwe, and had sat on a log with my paints beside me, only two or three yards from the precipice overlooking the gorge. The sun was scorching hot, so I wore only a shirt and shorts. While painting, I began to feel stings on my body and, lifting my shirt, saw ants all over me. Brushing off the ants I moved to another spot nearby. Hardly had I done so when a sudden cloud of spray, rising from the Falls, enveloped me and soaked the painting — with predictable results!

Living creatures themselves often prove a hazard. I had set up my easel and pastels by a pond in the Sussex countryside and was doing a landscape painting. The pond was beside a field, at the other end of which was a harmless herd of cows grazing. Time wore on and the cows grazed nearer and nearer. Just as my picture was near completion they all decided that they were thirsty and that I was standing where they wanted to drink. They finally came towards me tossing their heads and snorting until, almost too late, I got the message and in ignominious haste bundled my bits and pieces together and got out of their way.

On a recent visit to Sri Lanka I stood and painted a jungly landscape. Behind me was a fallen tree trunk on which I had rested the paints and water, and behind that the jungle. While I painted, huge Carpenter Bees kept flying noisily past, but I took little notice. After a while, however, their numbers and buzzing increased alarmingly. It soon became apparent that they had a nest in the log right behind me, hidden by tall grass. I decided that this was a wise moment to pack up! The picture had to be completed from memory.

Then there was that time in an Australian gum forest, when my father and I were making pastel drawings of the trees. It was an idyllic situation, apart from one big problem: flies! They made life a torment as they kept settling on our faces and on the drawings, and I marvel that we finished them. An insect repellent would undoubtedly have helped, but we hadn't remembered it!

CHAPTER 6

THE ART OF THE REID HENRYS

AN ASSESSMENT BY

DONALD WATSON

Bruce Henry. European Eagle Owl. Oil. 1982.

One day in the summer of 1960 George Henry arrived at our house in Galloway on his scooter — he was then nearly 70. I knew and greatly admired *A Guide to the Birds of Ceylon*, and it was a privilege to be able to ask him about his painting methods and to listen to his advice given with disarming modesty. He was eager to see a Peregrine (though he must have seen hundreds) and I remember his boyish delight when this was achieved after a short expedition. When he came back to Scotland at the age of 91, still active and alert as ever, I reminded him of that day and he instantly recalled that we had also seen a Short-eared Owl and a Ring Ouzel.

George Henry's nearest contemporaries among bird artists were Philip Rickman, Roland Green, J.C. Harrison and R.B. Talbot Kelly. Thorburn, Lodge and Liljefors were more than 20 years older. Looking again at his plates in *A Guide to the Birds of Ceylon* I am struck by the combination of liveliness and accuracy in his portraits of birds. His great experience of the living bird in its environment shines through on every page, and it is possible to sense his own joy in the beauty of so many species in the country where he lived so long. Some 40 years have passed since I saw the perky and colourful Red-vented Bulbul, for example, but George's illustration recaptures perfectly my remembered vision. The plate of Harriers (Colour Plate 13 in the present book) is full of the essence of Harrier flight and shows wonderful diversity of postures. It is true that it also shows one of his minor faults: a tendency at times to draw the head of a bird too large in proportion to the body. In this picture this is noticeable in the female Pallid Harrier. Nevertheless George Henry's birds are far more telling and truthful, in my view, than the regimented identification plates in many modern field guides. *Indian Peafowl, Ceylon Spurfowl and Ceylon Junglefowl* (Colour Plate 12) is an example of his skill in painting brilliant, irridescent feathering.

The special qualities in George's work which separate him from his contemporaries owe much to his upbringing in the countryside of Sri Lanka, with

G.M. Henry. Scorpion. Pen and ink.

its rich opportunities for the study of natural history. His entomological training, with continual microscopic work, obviously developed a natural eye for minutiae. Yet his sensitivity for form, light and·colour saved him from producing mere detailed maps of living creatures. One of the most arresting illustrations in this book is the superb *Metallic Beauties of Ceylon* (Colour Plate 3). This is a technical *tour de force* of gouache painting and must surely be unrivalled in its field. The shining colours of the insects have been superimposed on a white underpainting to maximise brilliance, and the background of unpainted grey paper is effectively chosen. *The Salticid Spider* (Colour Plate 8) and *Scorpion* (above) are other fine examples of entomological art.

A very different aspect of George's art is shown in pictures like the *Crested Barbet* (Colour Plate 6), painted in Africa in tempera, remarkably in his 87th year. The soft background and delicate, yet finely painted vegetation set the brightly plumaged bird convincingly in a natural environment. *Red Campion* (Colour Plate 7) is one of many charming flower studies done comparatively late in life in his favourite medium of tempera.

I have seen many delightful small landscape or foreground studies, painted directly from nature by George Henry in various mediums. He might use transparent water-colour for sky and distance, adding stronger foreground features in body-colour, or he would combine tempera and gouache in the same picture. In *Curlew, Oystercatchers, Ringed Plover and Turnstones* (Colour Plate 11) the tiny

G.M. Henry. Studies of a freshly dead Greenshank. Pencil. 1945.

G.M. Henry. Sleeping Mallard Duck. Pencil. 1947.

wavelets and sky-reflecting wet sand are indicated with great delicacy and observation. I like the small scale of the birds but sense some uncertainty in the artist's mind about their grouping and how much detail to give them — always problems in this kind of picture.

Charles Tunnicliffe's great series of measured drawings from dead birds received deserved acclaim. George Henry has left his own impressive legacy of work in this vein. In studies like those of the *Pallid Harrier* (page 99) his skill at modelling — recording every nuance of tonal value — produces a most satisfying reality. The detail is all there, not over stressed. Sometimes, as in the *Ceylon Black-headed Oriole* (Colour Plate 2), an accurate bird study becomes a stunning decoration. One of my favourites is the page of Greenshank drawings (page 86), including a marvellous, nearly head-on view into the bird's gape. Note too the care lavished on the drawing of a Wood Pigeon's feet, firmly grasping the branch (page 57).

G.M. Henry. Tempera studies of African Eagle Owl. 1977.

Any worthwhile wildlife artist who has spent a lifetime at his work accumulates thousands of pages of sketch-book drawings. These are always most interesting if they are truly field sketches, not carried further to please other eyes. In the *Sleeping Mallard Duck* (page 87) George of course wanted all the information it contains for his own use; while the Spotted Eagle Owl (page 53), Shelduck (page 89) and Merlins (page 90) are good examples of his quick drawing from life.

Soon after the end of the Second World War, David Reid-Henry was not only starting to illustrate major bird books but showing pictures at Roland Ward's gallery in Piccadilly. A reproduction of a Woodcock in a sombre woodland setting, painted at this time, lies before me as I write. Although clearly influenced by George Lodge and his own father's work, the style is already his own, remarkably crisp and highly finished. In the spring of 1950 David,

Oliver Heywood, James McEwan and I shared an exhibition at Roland Ward's. Our painting styles differed markedly. In a review David's was described as traditional, which was true enough; but few then realised that he would develop into the most masterly bird portraitist of his generation. In 1962, when he was internationally famous, particularly for his fine book plates, he told me of his disillusion with this kind of work. He was then staying with the Bannermans in Scotland and found it a hard struggle to complete the plates for *Birds of the Atlantic Islands*. Tiara was with him and he longed to be out in the hills flying her. He knew by then that he must escape the treadmill (as he saw it) of long series of book illustrations, and could only be content if he was free to paint as and when he chose. The great demand for his paintings had made this possible, and some of his very finest work was indeed done in Africa after he went to live there. To understand this it is only necessary to look at paintings like the *Sable Antelope* in Colour Plate 26. While I am not

G.M. Henry. Impressions of Sheldrake. Pen and ink. 1959.

G.M. Henry. Studies of a Jack Merlin. Pencil. 1954.

G.M. Henry. Unfinished study of Jack Merlin. Gouache. 1954.

qualified to comment from personal experience of the African scene I find this picture totally believable — hot sunlight, a closely studied acacia tree casting a cool shadow, termite mounds and the antelopes themselves, so beautifully scaled in the whole spacious landscape. How delightful is the touch of rufous colour on the animal's ear and the slight sheen of the same colour on the body!

As Bruce has said, a large part of David's life was lived in close association with his beloved falcons and eagles. I shall never forget arriving to see him one dark night when he was visiting Scotland, and being given my first sight of Tiara by torchlight in her temporary quarters in the Bannermans' barn. Lit up against the shadowy background, with the plumes of her great crest fanned out she was the

D.M. Henry. 'Baldie' - drawing of immature Peregrine, an early piece of work. Pencil.

most formidable bird I had ever seen. (See the portrait in Colour Plate 15.) David laughed, saying she was just 'a big Goshawk', but admitted she had recently torn out the jugular of an Alsatian which had unfortunately come within range of her terrible talons.

David was blessed with keen sight and also his father's eye for minutiae at close range, but even more importantly he was exceptionally good at seeing the essential modelling of his wildlife subjects. Look, for example, at the early (*circa* 1950) study of the Peregrine, Baldie (page 91) — the complex feather pattern is all there but it is rightly subordinated to the tonal modelling of the body. This is one area where lesser artists often fail in bird portraiture. The study of a *Verreaux's Eagle* (Colour Plate 16), painted in his maturity, is an even better and more subtle example of his skill in modelling birds in paint. Look particularly at how the underlying bone structure of the wing is indicated. This study has the special charm of an unfinished work. To some eyes David's paintings with birds in landscape settings appear too evenly finished. Bruce has explained (page 66) why David liked to keep everything in a picture 'in focus'. This is characteristic of the major colour plates he did for books like *Birds of the Atlantic Islands*. Some of his very finest illustrations of falcons, like those in *Eagles, Hawks and Falcons of the World*, have very little background.

Most wildlife artists have favourite subjects — one thinks of Lodge's falcons, Thorburn's game birds and small birds, Liljefors's Eider Ducks, Foxes and Hares. Sometimes, as with Thorburn's geese, a fine artist fails to get the proportions right in some other subjects. Although raptors were David's special birds it is remarkable how sure he was in the *drawing* of almost any bird or mammal. The *Nuthatch* (Colour Plate 18), the *European Bee-eater* (Colour Plate 23) and *Heuglin's Robin* (Colour Plate 24) are all prime examples of his skill in drawing and painting smaller birds. Even for his most routine book illustrations he spent time on careful

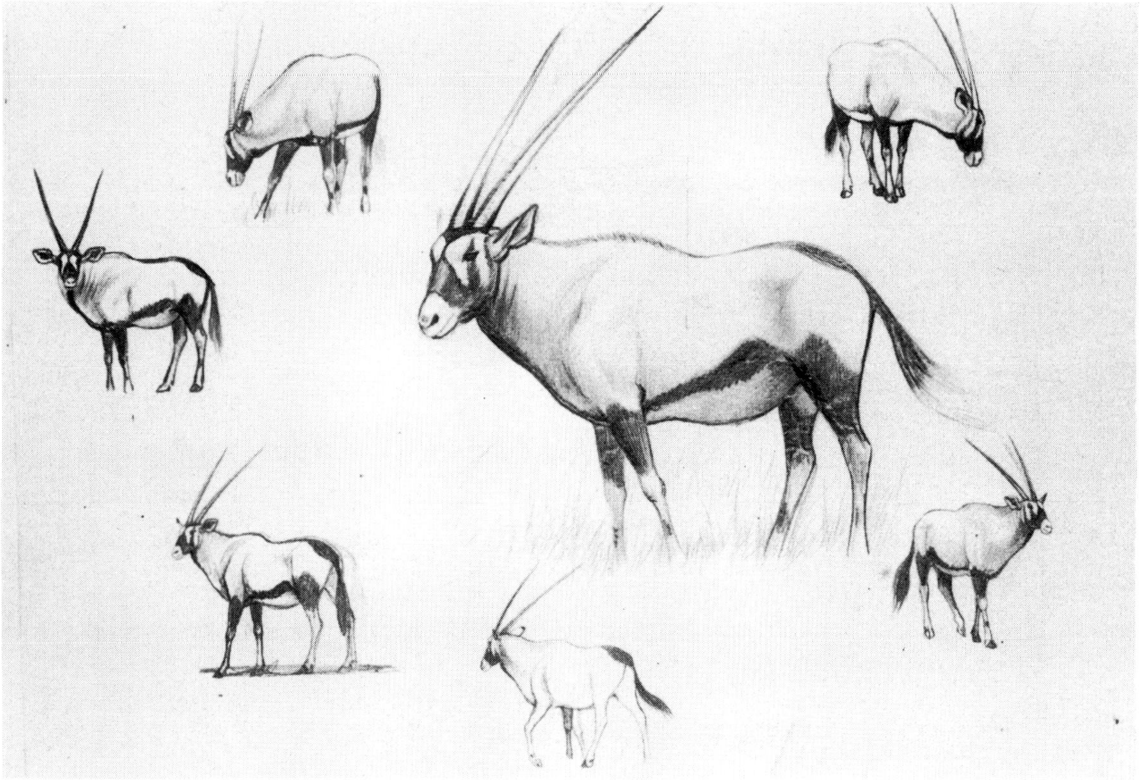

D.M. Henry. Gemsbok studies. Pencil.

preparation, selecting the most promising sketch and often tracing it direct for the final work. In addition to his colour work he did many fine black-and-white drawings for books. It is probably safe to say that he never allowed any work which fell short of his own exacting standards to leave his studio.

On page 40 Bruce reveals that David rarely took pencil and sketch-book into the field. It is extremely interesting to learn that the fine action drawings of a *Gemsbok (Oryx gazella) above* were probably done from fresh memory — although the delightful studies of *Red Bishops* (Colour Plate 19) were drawn from life. It is unusual for an animal artist to work without the aid of field sketches, but Joseph Crawhall's brilliantly free drawings of bullfights, for instance, depended on a similar combination of intense observation and memory drawing.

The *Lanner Falcon* (Colour Plate 25), painted in 1971, is perhaps unusual for David, in the bird being small-scaled in a large expanse of desert landscape. In his late years he clearly became more and more drawn to landscape painting — especially African landscapes — with the wildlife on a smaller scale. No doubt it can be said that some of his pictures in this manner come perilously close to photography. Had he lived another decade or so would he, like his father, have developed a less finished style? Possibly, but I cannot imagine him ceasing altogether to paint those magnificent close-ups of birds of prey, like the *Gyr Falcon* (Colour Plate 22), which above all else had made his name.

It could be said that Bruce is the most versatile artist of the three Henrys. He alone has worked frequently and on fairly large format in transparent water-colour. Apart from one example of boyhood work (page 95) everything he has in this book has been done in the last five years or so. He has of course painted intermittently throughout his life, but his special achievement has been in establishing himself as a high-quality wildlife artist after the age of 60, when he retired from his second career. His art, like that of his father and brother, has traditional roots and he has described his methods of working from preliminary sketches to thoroughly planned, finished pictures in Chapters 4 and 5. I have seen examples of his father's work done on location in Sri Lanka and Africa which show close affinity with some of Bruce's, but George lacked Bruce's confidence in tackling backgrounds or landscapes. Bruce modestly says, on page 39 , that the work he did to finish his father's picture of the *Ceylon Trogon* (Colour Plate 9) was cosmetic; but it is more than that, for the effectiveness of the picture owes a great deal to Bruce's splendid evocation of the jungle and deft introduction of the distant flying Trogon.

To my eye his Australian pastel of *The Three Sisters* (Colour Plate 40) is one of the most accomplished works in this book, which could not have been done by either of the others. The way in which the artist has captured the sunlight stealing across the landscape and the mysterious masses of

Bruce Henry. Mallards (painted when the artist was 17). Water-colour. 1935.

luminous shadow are just part of a remarkably atmospheric picture. I admire John Reaney's pastel landscapes with wildlife, but Bruce's succeed in a different style and seem close to paintings. This is especially true of *Beeches and Magpies at Arundel* (Colour Plate 39), an astonishingly vivid picture which could only have been done on the spot (apart from the birds).

The Highland painting expedition, described by Bruce on page 65, included stops in Galloway *en route* and on his way south. At that time I did not know him well and was a little anxious about how he would cope with the blizzards which were sweeping the north of Scotland. However, I need not have worried — he is a resourceful man. Anyone who has two careers behind him, then sets out at 60 to be a professional artist, has to be. From that short stay at

Torridon in arctic weather he brought back some very attractive, spontaneous pastels and water-colours which he would use for larger paintings when he returned to Sussex. The picture *Liathach from Loch Clair* (Colour Plate 36) arose, as he has described, from another trip to Torridon. It is a good example of traditional, very English water-colour 'drawing', in which he has used many cunning technical devices. Note the restrained colour scheme and how subtly the great mass of snow-streaked mountain is conveyed. The same skill at painting mountain scenery in water-colour appears in the ambitious '*Uneven Odds*' (Colour Plate 34). dominated by the Eagle in rapid flight. Perhaps the most delightful touch in this picture is the distant

Bruce Henry. Black Guillemot - sketches in Orkney. Pencil. 1984.

Bruce Henry. Studies of tame male Kestrel. Pencil. 1982.

Mountain Hare unmistakably running for its life. Nothing could be more wintry than *Goldeneyes at Loch Leven* (Colour Plate 31) — only in the hardest weather would such a group of Goldeneyes sit out on the ice. My initial reaction to this picture was that I would have liked the ducks to be rather less emphatic and detailed in such soft evanescent light. Certainly the landscape has a quite magical quality.

The water-colour of *'Fun on the Lek'* (Colour Plate 29) presents a scene which is very familiar to me. The birds have obviously been closely observed and are in authentic postures — the two sparring cocks are especially convincing. As always in Bruce's big expanses of landscape the distance is delightful but, artistically, the foreground does seem rather busy — though it is true that an even larger number of Black Game can be seen together at some leks.

When painting close-up pictures of just one or two birds Bruce often uses the convention of fading out the background (of course George and David also did this). It is a device which enables the artist to make essentially simple and pleasing compositions. In the two Sparrowhawk pictures (jacket, and Colour Plate 28) he has clearly set out to produce a simplified interpretation of a nest-site, and ornithologists who have watched Sparrowhawk nests may comment that they seem too open and at risk to the elements. None the less both pictures are drawn and painted with accomplishment, and the handling of the bird grasping the dead Song Thrush shows fine observation. Wrens with cocked tails have been painted so often that they invite cliché, but Bruce has managed a personal and delicate version of this subject (Colour Plate 35), both decorative and convincing. Using gouache he finds no problems in the bright colours and detail of the *Small Tortoiseshell on Buddleia* (Colour Plate 37) or the *Great Spotted Woodpeckers* (Colour Plate 32). These paintings show much affinity with his father's work.

It is good to see a range of Bruce's field sketches among the black-and-white illustrations. One of the most obvious lessons to be learned from good field sketches is that the shape of any one species of bird or mammal has no norm (as unfortunately it has to have in many identification guides). Look, for example, at the difference between the fat and the thin Kestrels on page 97.

Nowadays in exhibitions like the annual shows of the Society of Wildlife Artists there seem to be two main divergent trends. One is towards ever more sharply realised representation, the other towards an imaginative, even poetical, vision. Both have ardent admirers who may have no time for the other school. For some connoisseurs, animal art tends to stop at Audubon and the Chinese, with passing nods at Bewick, perhaps Crawhall and one or two others. Unfortunately, original works by great wildlife artists like Liljefors and Kuhnert are rarely on public view in Britain. Yet popular interest in paintings and illustrated books on wildlife has never been greater. The art of the Henry family is clearly basically of the representational kind, but there is surely enough variety of style and content in this book to please many different tastes.

G.M. Henry. Studies of a dead Pale (Pallid) Harrier, male (Circus macrourus). Gouache. 1945.

INDEX

(Page numbers printed in italics denote illustrations)